RKBA

rocks!

S Kie

SKIP
CORYELL

White Feather Press

Reaffirming Faith in God, Family, and Country!

BLOOD IN THE STREETS

Other Books by Skip Coryell

RKBA: Defending the Right to Keep and Bear Arms
Bond of Unseen Blood
Church and State
We Hold These Truths
Laughter and Tears

Available anywhere books are sold.

Signed copies are available only at
www.whitefeatherpress.com

Cover design created by Ron Bell of AdVision Design Group (www.advisiondesigngroup.com)

Third edition by White Feather Press in 2009

ISBN   978-0-9766083-3-2

Printed in the United States of America

Dedication

This book is dedicated to all those who guard the flock: to law enforcement, our military, and to CCW holders. God bless you all. Thank you for your service.

Acknowledgements and Thanks

Thank you to my friends: Ted Nugent, Sheriff Dar Leaf and all the officers of Barry County Michigan, to Sheriff Mark Denniston and all the officers of Jones County Iowa, Chuck Perricone and all of Michigan Coalition for Responsible Gun Owners (MCRGO), Sasha Nugent and all of Ted Nugent United Sportsmen of America (TNUSA), and to Craig Frank, Dave Neeson, Roger Burdette, Bobby Napier and Dave Stevens. All of you are sheep dogs with sharp teeth. You help guard my family, and I'll help guard yours.

And a special thanks to my good friend Ron Bell for designing the front and back covers of this book.

Foreword

The founding of the United States of America is a heroic story of how "God, guns, and guts" built the greatest bastion of liberty and prosperity that the world has ever seen.

On April 18, 1775, Paul Revere and William Dawes warned Concord and Lexington of the advance of the British troops. The British hoped to capture Samuel Adams and John Hancock in Lexington and seize the colonists' firearms and gunpowder at Concord, Massachusetts. The next day, the local farmers stood their ground at Old North Bridge in Concord.

> *By the rude bridge that arched the flood,*
> *Their flag to April's breeze unfurled;*
> *Here once the embattled farmers stood;*
> *And fired the shot heard round the world.*
> First Stanza of "Concord Hymn" by Ralph Waldo Emerson.

AMAZING! A bunch of armed farmers, who refused to give up their God-given rights, who knew how to use their firearms, and who prepared for armed combat took on the greatest military power of their day and . . . You know the rest.

> *In the books you have read*
> *How the British Regulars fired and fled,—*
> *How the farmers gave them ball for ball,*
> *From behind each fence and farmyard wall,*
> *Chasing the redcoats down the lane,*

Then crossing the fields to emerge again
Under the trees at the turn of the road,
And only pausing to fire and load.

From the "Midnight Ride of Paul Revere" by Henry Wadsworth Longfellow.

Since that time, over two million service men and women have been injured or killed to protect our freedom. Unfortunately, we tend to forget the past and its hard-learned lessons. When we take our liberty for granted our God-given rights gradually erode.

For too long, the liberal media and the gun-grabbing politicians have told the American people that a civilized society has no need for firearms—after all, the police are here to protect us. The liberal media and the gun-grabbing politicians are wrong!

What happens when the window shatters in your home at night? Is it a sex predator wanting to rape your daughter? Is it a crazed dope addict high on drugs? You need a gun and you need it NOW!

Certainly the government would never turn on its citizens and abuse its power, would it? Tell that to the African Americans, the Jewish Americans, and the Catholic Americans of 100 years ago when the KKK ran the local and state governments in much of the United States.

Leftwing politicians that want to confiscate our firearms also want to cut and run from the Islamofascist terrorists in the Middle East. If they have their way, how are law-abiding citizens to respond when terrorists attack us in the streets?

Think it can't happen here?

Tell that to the students of the University of North Carolina at Chapel Hill where Mohammed Reza Taheri-azar on March 3, 2006, deliberately drove his rented Jeep into a heavily-trafficked pedestrian area on campus, injuring nine people, because he wanted to "avenge the deaths or murders of Muslims around the world."

Tell that to the Jewish Americans in Seattle, Washington where Naveed Afzal Haq, on July 28, 2006, shot and killed Pamela Waechter and wounded five others at the Jewish Federation of Greater Seattle because he was "a Muslim American angry at Israel".

Tell that to the pedestrians in San Francisco, California where Omeed Aziz Popal, on August 29, 2006, deliberately ran down and killed Stephen Jay Wilson and injured 14 other pedestrians with his SUV because "Everyone needs to be killed."

Don't trust the liberals. Don't trust their mushy-headed reasoning. Don't trust their feel-good motives. Tell them to keep their hands off our guns.

In Michigan we have been able to retrieve most of our Second Amendment rights. Michigan is now a "shall issue" state. Michigan has also enacted the "stand your ground" law. But more needs to be done. Why should the law prevent us from protecting ourselves in our day care centers, our schools, our churches, and our sports arenas?

Educate yourself. Read the history of the American Revolution and the other great wars where citizens fought for liberty against tyranny. Read why Hitler did not invade Switzerland in World War II. Read how gun owners deposed a corrupt political machine by force in Athens, Tennessee in 1946.

You need to be involved. Join the National Rifle Association and a good state gun owners association like the Michigan Coalition for Responsible Gun Owners (MCRGO). Ask questions of your elected officials—all the way from the Sheriff to the President. If your elected officials don't trust you with your firearms, vote them out of office. Support candidates who respect your rights.

Most importantly, ask educators what they are teaching your children about their constitutional rights and obligations, and especially about the Second Amendment. If their school is teaching "political correctness" or "diversity" instead of history and civics, put them in a school that teaches the importance of our Constitution. Teach your children how to use a gun safely and effectively. Their freedom depends on it.

And now, as you read Skip Coryell's book "Blood in the Streets" please remember the great heritage that our forefathers fought and bled and died for, and then passed on to us. Skip's book was written with that same spirit: the spirit of freedom and the spirit of "God, guns, and guts"! Read on and remember.

*— Alan Cropsey, Michigan State Senator and
MCRGO Board of Directors —*

Introduction

I'm just the Sheriff, so I'm going to keep this simple. I haven't written anything more creative than a police report in a long time, but after reading Skip's book and getting the invitation to be a part of it, I had to take him up on it. I want to help. Skip and I have been friends for many years, and I trust his character. We both have many things in common. We love God, our family and our country. That will never change.

In this book, Skip talks about sheep, wolves, and sheep dogs. I am a sheep dog, and I have dedicated my life to law enforcement. It is my job to guard honest, law abiding citizens (despite the "Warren v. District of Columbia landmark case that says police have no legal obligation to protect civilians) And I do that even if it means sacrificing my own life. That's what sheep dogs are all about. We willingly put ourselves in harm's way even if it means not coming home at night to our wife and kids. I hate the thought of that, but it's a reality. It's part of the job.

I respect Skip and the other CCW holders who are also willing to sacrifice their lives for the innocent. I thank you all very much. You are a rare breed, but a necessary one. Us cops need all the help we can get. It seems like society is going a little crazy these days with all the drugs, the mental illness, and the breakdown in our moral fabric. I'm no sociologist. Like I said before, I'm just the Sheriff, but I can tell you that the streets out there are dangerous.

But here's the whole point of what I want to say. Carrying a concealed pistol for protection is not about killing. It's about love for your fellow man. It was Jesus Christ who said: "Greater love has no man than to lay down his life for a friend." And when a CCW holder straps on a sidearm, he or she is making a commitment to help us cops guard the flock. They have become part of the solution.

There is evil in the world, and it must be opposed. So I encourage you to read Skip Coryell's book and consider joining the ranks of police officers, our military, and our civilian CCW holders. We're all on the same team. We guard the flock. We oppose the scum. We take out the trash.

Get training. Get prepared. Complete the transition from sheep to sheepdog, from defenseless victim to a guardian of the innocent. And remember, a sheep has the right to live, but it has no self respect. Like Skip says:

> *"Sheep are born and bred for one purpose: to be killed and to have their parts processed into something useful by predators. They stand on the hill and go "Baa", as they're being slaughtered."*

Don't say "Baa". Say "Stop or I'll shoot!" The choice is yours.

— Dar Leaf, Barry County Sheriff and NRA
Training Counselor —

"Let me get this straight: Running, crying, whimpering, and hiding under desks and pews? You mean to say that when an imbecile walks into a church, office, a day care center, or school, stumbling about, almost zombie-like, with gun-filled hands at his side, blabbering incoherently to his next victim, the reaction of grown men and women is to run, cry, whimper, and hide under a desk or pew? The sheeping of America is nearly complete."

— Ted Nugent —

Welcome to the Party Pal!

"There'll be Blood in the Streets! Road rage! Shootouts in public! It'll be like Dodge City all over again!"

Yeah. Sure. And the sky is falling too. Such were the hysterical cries in my home state of Michigan when the anti-Second Amendment crowd was fighting to prevent Michigan's CCW, shall-issue legislation from being passed. You'd think we were trying to legalize baby killing! Oh, that's right. It's already legal to kill babies in America; it's called abortion. But then I digress.

That has been the unsubstantiated claim in every state who has ever passed shall-issue CCW legislation: "Blood in the Streets". Okay, it's been six years. Where's the blood? That's odd. I don't see it. It's not in the paper; it's not in the streets. With all the stink made from the far left opposed to CCW, we should be drowning in blood by now. Our streets should be stained by the bright, crimson tide. But it's not there. Hmmm, maybe they were wrong? Do ya think so?

And now, even as I write this chapter, I hear about all the fuss over in our neighboring state of Wisconsin, as they fight year after year, trying desperately to pass their own shall-issue CCW bill into law. (And while I'm thinking about it, congratulations and a hearty salute to Kansas and Nebraska on your new CCW law. Good job!)

"Blood in the streets! We're all going to die! It's the end of the world as we know it!"

After 39 states have passed shall-issue laws, you'd think the anti-Second Amendment crowd could come up with a better argument, but they haven't, and they can't. That's the problem with defending an indefensible position. You are doomed to failure before the first shot is fired – pun intended. It's gotten to the point where their hysterical cries are laughable.

So that's the myth. That's the fallacy. That's the out and out lie of CCW. But what is the truth? The media won't tell you. They don't want you to know. But why? Why do they want a population of unarmed and defenseless sheep?

The immortal words of Rhett Butler (Clark Gable) from the movie *"Gone with the Wind"* come to mind: "Frankly, my dear, I don't give a damn!"

People keep asking me "why?". I no longer care. I no longer give the time of day to every idiot with a political axe to grind. But then they say, "You should be more tolerant of other people's ideas. You should expand your mind."

I've got a better idea. Maybe they should reach back and pull their own minds out of their rectums and see the world for what it really is – Dangerous! Always has been –always will be. It's human nature.

My friend and mentor, Ted Nugent, put it like this in his own book *"God, Guns, and Rock-n-roll"*:

"Let me get this straight: Running, crying, whimpering, and hiding under desks and pews? You mean to say that when an imbecile walks into a church, office, a day care center, or school, stumbling about, almost zombie-like, with gun-filled hands at his side, blabbering incoherently to his next victim, the reaction of grown men and women is to run, cry, whimper, and hide under a desk or pew? The sheeping of America is nearly complete."

I don't think so! Not this good ole boy! Where is the anger America? Where's the outrage? Where's the attitude? Shoot back! Fight back! Pull your cowardly, mangy carcass out from under the table and shoot to stop the threat! Where is your manhood? Where are your cajones! You'd better reach down and check to make sure they're still there! Cuz if ya don't use 'em, you'll lose 'em!

There is already blood in the streets! Gang members shooting each other; drive by shootings; wolves mugging sheeple-people with impunity! America used to be characterized by people who stood up and fought for what was right! Where did that attitude go? Where are the potential sheep dogs who would guard the flock? Stand by for change, or, as Ted would call it, "Upgrade!"

I'll tell you where they are: they're hiding beneath a thin, artificial veneer of political correctness and tolerance. But listen to me, sheeple! Some things were never meant to be tolerated! Robbery, graft, corruption, murder, rape. We can no longer afford to put up with those things here in America. As of this writing, there are over 150,000 sheep dogs in my home state of Michigan. We're licensed by the government and we're called CCW holders. That's a pretty good start. But we need more. Bad-guy-criminal scum beware! The good people of America are righteously angry, armed, and ready to fight back! And NRA Instructors like myself and the good Sheriff Leaf are teaching them how to do it! It's time to take out the trash! Meth cookers beware! Gangbangers get off the streets! Drug dealers repent and change your ways while you still can! It's "come to Jesus time" for everyone!

It's time to wake up and smell the "Blood in the Streets", because the blood has always been there, and it will always be around. But all the utopian peacemongers in our society stand up and cry out from their ivory towers with one, loud, naïve voice: "Can't we all just get along?"

Give me a break! And let's all just join hands and circle the campfire, singing endless verses of "Kumbaya". Oops! What's wrong with this picture? The guy holding my hand wants to steal my wallet to buy drugs. The guy 5 sheeple down wants to kidnap my son. The sixth person to my left wants to rape my wife. Hmmm, I guess maybe we can't all "just get along" after all. Reality always gets in the way of utopia, and reality will always be trump.

Would I like to live forever in peace and harmony? Yes. Will it ever happen? No, not until we reach Heaven. I have a friend who believes that all people are inherently good. I don't blame him. He wants to feel safe. He has a positive personality, always looking for the good in everyone. To a degree, that's a good thing. But I remember that on nine-eleven my friend was shattered. Someone had plugged the holes in his bowling ball and there was nothing left for him to grab onto. I remember him asking me: "How could people do such a thing?" I felt sorry for him, but I also wanted to reach around and manually pull his head out of his butt. What a terrible mess that would have been.

I was abhorred and revolted by nine-eleven, but it didn't surprise me. I was saddened at the loss of life, but I was equally outraged. One of my favorite Christmas movies is "*Diehard*" with Bruce Willis. Yes, I know. It's not really a Christmas movie, but just humor me for a moment. Do you remember the part where John McClane (Bruce Willis) was trapped inside the Nakatomi building and he was trying to get help from the outside world and no one would listen to him? He pulled a fire alarm; that didn't work. He dialed 911; that didn't work. Finally, he dropped the dead body of a terrorist onto a police cruiser. Then he very nonchalantly exclaimed to the retreating police officer, "Welcome to the party, pal." That worked!

To my naïve friend, and all other misguided people who maintain that humans are inherently good, I point to nine-eleven and exclaim, "Welcome to the party, pal!" There are people out there, wolves, who want to kill you and your family. Are you going to let them? Go ahead if you want to, but as for me and my house, we're going to fire for effect, and double-tap the center of exposed mass! This is no time in history to be a wussy.

And, if you still stubbornly believe that people are inherently good, then try to reason it out this way:

Inherently means: ADJECTIVE: Existing as an essential constituent or characteristic; intrinsic.

Intrinsic: ADJECTIVE: Of or relating to the essential nature of a thing; inherent.

Here's a news flash! Goodness is not the essential nature of humanity. If that were true, then there would be no crime, no need for laws, no need for police, etc. People would intrinsically know what is right and wrong and the natural desire of their heart would be to "do good". But it's not. People do bad. And even those of us who resist the temptation of evil, we still harbor secret desires of greed, lust, and violence. Even the best humanity has to offer needs the accountability of law and its corresponding punishment. Else, they will fall into that "human", downward spiral of graft and corruption.

And that's the way it is, folks! I don't know how else to break it to you. People are bad. Some people are really bad! Some are downright evil incarnate. Now for the rest of you, those who didn't close the book after my first paragraph, you must now be feeling pretty helpless. You're probably scared to death. "What! I'm in danger! People are bad? People want to hurt me? Oh no! The sky is falling! We're all going to die!"

Shut up and relax before I slap you. Let me encourage you. All is not lost. I want you to run out and take an NRA Personal Protection in the Home Course. Then get yourself a Glock .40 caliber semi automatic with some dependable premium self defense rounds. Corbons and Hydrashocks are both good, and then . . . no more problem! In the immortal words of Colonel Hackworth, God rest his soul, "Stay alert –stay alive"!

But, if you still insist on remaining a helpless sheep, cowering in a puddle of your own urine, then go ahead. I'll protect your worthless carcass. After all, I'm a sheep dog. That's what I do. But don't you dare try and take away my teeth. Cuz if you do, I will rip your hand off! Have a nice day, and drive safely.

"We were surrounded by Chinese soldiers for two days. They always attacked at dawn, always blowing those bugles, and it made my skin crawl to hear them coming. We kept killing them, but they kept coming."

A Time to Kill - A Time to Die

After that first chapter, half of you are probably cheering, saying, "Yes! Someone finally said what I've been thinking!" The rest of you are, no doubt, starting to believe that I'm a blood-and-guts, war-mongering maniac, impatient to shoot the first bad guy who crosses my path. Kind of like Dirty Harry, "Go ahead, make my day!"

Well, all of that might be true, but the only way for you to find out for sure is to keep on reading. I gotcha now! Your day is mine!

But once again, I digress. What was I talking about? Oh yes, "Go ahead, make my day!" Let's get serious for a moment. In my experience with CCW holders (as an NRA Instructor, I have taught about a thousand of them) they never "want" to pull the trigger. Sometimes they are forced to, but they never desire it, and they never enjoy it. When I teach the NRA Personal Protection in the Home Course, I tell my students this: "There are only two ways to flunk this class. (NRA classes are not designed to flunk people, they are designed to teach people.) First, if you exhibit a pattern of poor safety on the range, you'll be asked to come back and work with me some more until you've replaced those unsafe habits with safe ones. Secondly, anyone who talks about blowing another person away, even jokingly, will not receive an NRA certificate from me. In addition to that, I'll turn your name into the local gun board, and you'll never sued a concealed pistol license in this county.

A firearm is a tool of last resort, and should be used only to protect an innocent life from imminent death or great bodily injury. Having said that, out of the vast number of students I've taught, only one has been asked to come back because of poor safety habits, and no one has exhibited an aggressive or nonchalant attitude concerning firearms. Firearms can be fun, but they are also a very serious matter.

Many of my students share with me that they leave the class with one overwhelming prayer in their mind: "Dear God, I hope I never have to unholster my pistol." I share that prayer with them. I am a sheep dog, but I am also human. I believe that "normal" people have a natural aversion to killing another of their own kind.

For myself, I have never had to kill another person. Indeed, although I'm an avid deer hunter (killed six just behind the house last year) I still feel a bit of remorse at the taking of an animal's life. The taking of an animal's life is a reverent act, one that I do often, but with all due honor and respect. In my first novel, "Bond of Unseen Blood" this principle is explained in detail, so I won't elaborate on it now.

Any "normal" person who has been forced to kill another human, knows the adverse effects it can have on you. I back this up with conversations I've had with many combat veterans of all ages. Most vets who have had to kill, are loathe to speak of it.

Case in point, I give you my own father, who served as an Air Force Ranger in the Korean War. His job was to parachute behind enemy lines and destroy radar and communications installations. He called it electronics counter espionage. It all sounded very glamorous to a kid, but now, I realize that there was no glamour in it at all, only pain, and suffering, and death.

My father rarely talked about his experiences there, but I remember on one particular occasion he did so with extraordinary detail, imagery and passion. I'll recount his story as I remember it.

"We were surrounded by Chinese soldiers for two days. They always attacked at dawn, always blowing those bugles, and it made my skin crawl to hear them coming. We kept killing them, but they kept coming. We were running out of ammunition, but we had plenty of explosives, so we made cannons out of pipes, and shot rocks, metal, glass, anything that we could find at them. On the last day, right after the dawn attack, a few of the survivors said that I ran off after the retreating Chinese, shooting them as I went. They followed the trail of dead bodies and found me sitting on the ground staring off into space, covered in dirt and blood. I don't remember any of it, and later, after being shot in the leg, I was sent home on a submarine. The Air Force sent me to a psychiatrist, but he said I would get over it. I slept with my eyes open for months after the battle."

But my father didn't get over it, and, after hearing his story, I never looked at him in quite the same way again. He always seemed a little more dangerous to me after that. I suspect if more kids had a little bit of fear in them, they might turn out as better citizens. Instead, they're spoiled. Whenever I see one of those "NO FEAR" bumper stickers on the back of some young kid's car, I just want to pull him over and start slapping some sense into him. Fear is a good thing. It inspires courage.

"Skip's book references the Korean War many times. My father, John Humphrey, and Skip's father, Jerome Coryell, fought in that miserable Korean War. Our fathers' sacrifice for freedom is one of our greatest blessings."

—M. Carol Bambery — NRA Board of Directors, MCRGO Foundation President

Now where was I? Oh yes. Because I reverence all life, especially humans who possess souls, I avoid using my pistol at all costs, short of allowing an innocent life to be taken.

Here's what I tell my students:

All of you will live or die based on the decisions you make. It's that way through all of life, not just with firearms. If you don't act, you may die, or you may carry the guilt of inaction the rest of your life. If you act when you should not, you may die anyways, or you may spend some time in jail. In any event, the very act of shooting or not shooting is a life-changing event. You will never be the same.

After that, the inevitable question remains: "How do I know when I should shoot?"

That's not an easy question to answer, because the answer is different for everyone. Every situation, and every person, is different. We all have different abilities, different mindsets, different religious convictions, and all these things must be taken into account before we decide when to shoot. Of course, the time to decide is beforehand, because after a person points a gun in your face, it's too late for a moral decision-making process. There just isn't the time. Ahhh, so many bullets, so little time.

Pardon my earthy tastes, but I like the movie "Roadhouse" with Patrick Swayze and Sam Elliott. Swayze's character is agonizing over having killed a man several years earlier. Sam looks at him, straight in the eye, and answers him point blank: "When a man sticks a gun in your face, you got two choices: You can kill the f$%#er, or you can die!"

I guess that about sums it up. But, like I said, it's a personal decision, and all of us have to make that decision for ourselves. Shooting is a decision, just as not shooting is also a decision.

Francis Schaeffer, a popular religious writer in the latter part of the twentieth century once wrote a book titled: "How Shall We Then Live?" In it, he explored how God would have us live our short lives here on earth. I believe it's the same with CCW holders. All of us will ultimately decide one of two things: "How shall we then live?" or conversely, "How shall we then die?"

To illustrate the point, let me tell you about a student I once had. I was teaching a husband and wife in a private lesson on their farm in southwest Michigan. We were on the range behind their barn, shooting at targets up against an embankment.

The woman was shooting a nice, 9mm Glock, and she honestly could not hit the broad side of a barn from the inside.

I tried everything I knew to get her on target, but it was no use. I couldn't find the problem. Her husband told me she was a good shot, and that she usually shot better than him, so he didn't understand the problem either. I questioned her some more, and she finally threw up her hands in frustration and said, "I don't even know why I'm doing this! I could never shoot anyone anyways. My husband made me take this class!"

At her remark, a light went off in my head, and I interjected. "What if someone was trying to kill you? Could you shoot someone then?"

She said, "No! I couldn't kill someone to save my own life. I'd just go ahead and die!"

I thought that was rather odd, but I could tell she was sincere, so I thought about it a second. Even though most people have an aversion to killing another human, I personally believe that there are very few people on this planet who would rather die than protect themselves. Almost everyone has a point where they will cross the line and take a life.

Earlier in the day, this couple had introduced me to their baby girl, so I said,

"How old is your daughter?"

"Nine months."

"Okay, let's use a little training technique called visualization."

She nodded her head impatiently.

"Okay, here's the scenario: You're at the gas station filling your tank. A man drives up and parks next to your car. He gets out, walks over, reaches through the open window of your car, removes your daughter from her car seat and puts her in his own car. He then starts to get into his car to drive away."

There was a horrified look on the young mother's face.

"At that moment in time, could you take another human life?"

She said, "I would kill that son of a bitch!"

I said, "Okay then, that target down there is that man who is stealing your daughter. Fire away."

She never missed the target again.

That real-life event inspired chapter 23 of my novel "*We Hold These Truths*".

But like I said, we all have to live and die based on our own decisions. For me, I decided like this:

I have two children, ages 9 and 11. If I'm sitting in McDonald's with my family, and a man walks in and starts shooting, I would have no choice but to defend myself, my family, and the family of everyone in that building. It would impact me. I would feel bad about killing someone. I may even need some therapy for a while.

However, Freud himself couldn't assuage my guilt if I sat there and allowed a man to walk from person to person while I stood idly by and let him kill innocent people. I would never recover. I would feel guilt-ridden for the rest of my life. I couldn't live with myself - and rightly so.

I believe that with great power comes great responsibility, and a .40 caliber Smith and Wesson is a lot of power. I believe it's my duty as a fellow human being to protect the innocent lives of others. I believe individually, and, as a society, we are all honor-bound to protect those who are unable to protect themselves. It is our solemn duty as humans.

Here's the deal: You help protect my family, and I'll help protect yours. It's the human thing to do. It's the only thing that makes sense to this Marine Corps father.

There are verses in the Bible (Ecclesiastes 3:1-3) which say:

"To everything there is a season, and a time to every purpose under Heaven: A time to be born, and a time to die; a time to plant, and a time to pluck up that which is planted; a time to kill, and a time to heal; a time to break down, and a time to build up."

Again I reiterate, that a firearm is a tool of last resort. But even God recognizes that there is a time to kill. You decide the time. Both God and man will judge your decision. Better be right.

But remember this one thing: if you don't survive, then nothing else matters.

I leave you with the closing words of a great American hero, a sheepdog who dedicated his life to guarding the flock.

"I'm a sheepdog. I live to protect the flock and confront the wolf. If you have no capacity for violence then you are a healthy productive citizen, a sheep. If you have a capacity for violence and

no empathy for your fellow citizens, then you have defined an aggressive sociopath, a wolf. But what if you have a capacity for violence, and a deep love for your fellow citizens? What do you have then? A sheepdog, a warrior, someone who is walking the hero's path. Someone who can walk into the heart of darkness, into the universal human phobia, and walk out unscathed."

—LTC(RET) Dave Grossman, RANGER, Ph.D., author of "On Killing."—

Now, go with God. Guard the sheep. It's your duty.

Was I going to be arrested? Was I breaking the law by entering? I didn't know. I didn't care. I just knew I was doing the right thing, so I forged on ahead. I was Rosa Parks with a video camera! "Get out of my way Michael Moore! Here I come!"

Rednecks and Rabblerousers

Without grassroots activism, there would be no CCW laws - for anyone. In fact, there would be no Second Amendment at all. One could even expand that to say: "there would be no America." Because, after all, America was founded by a bunch of rednecks and rabble rousers who thought they knew better than the king of the mightiest nation on the planet.

Samuel Adams, one of the lesser known founders of our country, was also one of my favorites. I'm convinced he was a redneck and a rabble rouser, and Jeff Foxworthy backs me up on it as well in one episode of his sitcom "*The Jeff Foxworthy Show*". Jeff put it like this:

"Some of our greatest leaders have been rednecks. Why you take for instance, Samuel Adams. Any guy with a beer named after him – redneck!"

Sam Adams was such an instigator. He had a knack for enflaming the public, and then standing by and watching as they burned King George in effigy, or tossed tons of tea into Boston Harbor. Yeah, good ole Sam. He was my kind of guy. He was a good ole boy with a New England accent.

Years ago, when I first became involved in Ted Nugent United

Sportsmen of America (TNUSA), I too became "that kind of guy". The first issue I tackled was the CCW bill that then State Representative Alan Cropsey was trying to get passed into law. The "anti's" had dug their heels in, and the bill was going nowhere. I was just an Area Director at the time, so I decided to tackle my own home county first.

I remember, that at that time, I was working on my second failed marriage. I was a miserable man with an axe to grind, and I was in no mood for morons. But, we had an anti-CCW Sheriff, so I started there. My misery fueled my soul with courage and boldness. I had balls of solid rock!

I remember my first convert to the cause was Dave Neeson. He called me on the phone and said he wanted to get involved. I had made a hundred phone calls to TNUSA members, and he was the only one to volunteer his time. So, full of piss and vinegar and not to be thwarted or discouraged, I set up a time to meet Dave at the Hastings McDonald's for coffee.

When I got there, I was surprised when Dave rolled through the door in a wheelchair. My heart sank. I was going to take on the County Sheriff, the County Prosecutor, and the Michigan State Police (i.e., the County Gun Board) with just myself and a "cripple"? But that's the commonality with all grassroots movements; they always start with a single concerned citizen. And, being the optimist that I was, I forged on ahead. After careful thought, I was encouraged. I had just doubled the size of the movement. Now there were two of us – a force to be reckoned with.

Later on I came to realize that Dave was not crippled at all. I was the cripple, and it was my own ignorance, lack of experience, and limited thinking that handicapped me. Since then, I have come to know Dave as the tallest man on two wheels and a force to be reckoned with. But then, once again, I digress.

Dave and I made plans to crash the next County Gun Board meeting which was held at the local State Police Post. For years, the gun board had violated state law (the Michigan 'Open Meetings Act') by holding their meetings in a secured, locked-down facility, closed to the public. That was the first thing we had to change. I had spoken earlier to Mike Hoban and Mike Carson from another Second Amendment group called Brassroots. They told me of the success they had gained with several other counties by videotaping the gun board meetings. It put the board under a microscope and made them feel more accountable to the law and to the people.

But how was I going to videotape them if I couldn't get into the meetings? Dave and I had it all figured out.

On the day of the meeting, we were waiting in Dave's pickup truck in the State Police parking lot. Neither of us owned a camera, so Dave borrowed one from a friend. It was a relic, a big, shoulder-mounted antique that looked more like an anti-tank weapon than a camera. The great video beast must have weighed 38 pounds field dressed.

As was their custom, the State Police Commander walked out into the parking lot to get the next CCW candidate and escort him in through the locked doors. As soon as he turned around to walk back in, I jumped out of the truck with the giant camera on my right shoulder and ran up behind him. He never turned around. The front door was under construction, so he took the candidate around back and through the locked door. I caught the door before it closed and walked in right behind them, my eye fixed to the eyepiece, camera rolling all the while.

Was I going to be arrested? Was I breaking the law by entering? I didn't know. I didn't care. I just knew I was doing the right thing, so I forged on ahead. I was Rosa Parks with a video camera! "Get out of my way Michael Moore! Here I come!"

We walked down a corridor. A State Trooper passed me and stared. But he didn't stop me. Why should he? I was coming in right behind his boss. I walked into the conference room and sat down beside the Commander. That was the first time he noticed I was there. He and the Under-sheriff looked up together. Their eyes got as big as donuts, then they looked back down again.

Much to my surprise, they never spoke to me or even acknowledged my presence. That was weird. The meeting lasted 90 minutes and they never even looked at me again. They just ran the meeting the way they always had, with one very important exception. Under the scrutiny of that giant camera orb, they issued an unrestricted CCW permit.

To this day, I remember the look of shock on the CCW candidate's face when they voted unanimously to issue him an unrestricted concealed pistol license. I didn't know the man, but he had already been denied twice, so he just kept coming back over and over again on principle. He said to them, "You are? You're going to give me one this time?" It was funny to watch, but also very satisfying. I remember his name was Bob.

After the meeting was over, I got up and sauntered out without saying a word. I was on top of the world. Later on we surmised that they had mistaken me for a local TV station, probably due in part to the size of my camera. Well, who knows, maybe bigger is better.

Dave and I celebrated, but were disappointed to realize that the camera didn't work. I had gone in there as brazen as John Wayne, packing a dead camera on my shoulder. Oh well, it was a beginning. The mission was accomplished.

Our movement snowballed. We wrote letters to the Editor. We

allied with a local group called B-SAFR, Barry County Citizens for Second Amendment and Firearms Rights, founded by Dave Stevens. Dave had already been working hard in support of CCW reform, even before me.

Brazen as a Grizzly bear, I sent the gun board the following letter. It was to be my proverbial "shot across the bow". As it turned out, it was the calm before the storm and the peaceful lull before the battle.

To: Barry County Gun Board
From: Skip Coryell, SW Michigan Director, Ted Nugent United Sportsmen of America
Date: 23 April 2000

My name is Skip Coryell, a resident of Barry County, and the Director of Ted Nugent United Sportsmen of America (TNUSA) for the following counties in Michigan: Barry, Allegan, Calhoun, Van Buren, Kalamazoo, Branch, Berrien, Cass, and St. Joseph. While it is our long-term goal to achieve CCW reform for all counties in Michigan, we have decided to start with the above-mentioned counties in SW Michigan.

With the support of many local, state, and national pro-hunting and second amendment organizations, TNUSA has decided to work toward reforming the way Concealed Weapons Permits are issued in Barry County.

It is our firm belief that Barry County citizens are being denied their constitutional right to "keep and bear arms for the defense of themselves and the state." Presently, the Barry County Gun Board does not issue CCW permits for the reason of personal and family defense. In fact, the gun board issues very few general CCW permits, turning most people down because they cannot demonstrate what the board believes to be adequate need. When I picked up my own CCW application, a government employee advised me, "Save your 50 dollars. We don't issue CCW permits in Barry County." There seems to be one exception to this rule: retired police officers are given general permits with no questions asked, and are not even required to appear before the board.

However, we believe that the right to keep and bear arms is a God-given, inalienable right, which is incapable of being surrendered or transferred, regardless of any temporary political power (e.g., the Barry County Gun Board). An inalienable right, by nature, transcends space and time. It cannot be contained within any human law, written or otherwise, because it was endowed to us by our Creator, who is Himself the embodiment of morality and all that is right and good. Furthermore, an inalienable right is one bestowed upon all people, not just one class of citizen, such as retired police officers. This practice is elitist, and endangers the very foundations of liberty. We are all entitled to equal protection under the law.

We believe that demanding proof of adequate need, a policy which is intrinsically subjective and relative, is ludicrous and in violation of the very tenets and principles on which our country was founded. The 10 amendments that comprise the Bill of Rights were never intended by our founding fathers to require "proof of adequate need." Otherwise, we would be required to demonstrate adequate need before practicing other constitutionally guaranteed rights, such as freedom of religion or freedom of speech. One only has to read "The Federalist Papers" or the personal correspondence of people like Thomas Jefferson, George Washington, and Alexander Hamilton in order to glean the true intent of the Bill of Rights. Imagine the Hastings Banner being shut down by the government, because they could not demonstrate sufficient need to publish their news and editorials. Or imagine a church being closed by the county because they can survive without worshipping God. The Bill of Rights was written to prevent an ever-intrusive government from encroaching on the personal rights of its citizens. Ironically enough, the Bill of Rights was written to protect citizens from their own government. The founding fathers knew human nature, and guaranteed us this protection against a corrupt, totalitarian government. For this principle they shed their blood, fought, and died. We are forever in their debt, and we thank them.

However, the Barry County Gun Board may argue that they are merely protecting honest, law-abiding citizens from themselves and from one other, but this, too, is ludicrous and fundamentally flawed for the following reason: "An honest- law-abiding citizen does not need protection from another honest, law-abiding citizen." By definition, honest, law-abiding citizens do not commit crimes. However, we do need protection from criminals because, by definition, criminals are those who are dishonest and do not abide by the law. Law enforcement agencies, however well-intentioned, cannot and should not be everywhere, lest we end up with a police state.

The present Gun Board policy leaves responsible,

law-abiding citizens to fend for themselves, primarily defenseless, like sheep without a shepherd, simply waiting passively for the wolves. But we are no longer content to passively chew our cuds and wait for the wolves, hoping above hope that our wives and children do not become victims. Because of this, we will use all legal and political means to persuade you to begin issuing general CCW permits to honest, responsible and well-trained, law-abiding citizens who wish to carry concealed weapons for personal and family defense. We petition the Gun Board to establish written guidelines and requirements, thereby making general CCW permits attainable for personal and family protection.

In conclusion, let us say that while this transition may seem uncomfortable; it is a change that must occur if we are to protect our families and friends. However, we pledge to make this transition as quick and painless as possible for all parties concerned. We assure you that our differences are purely philosophical, and that nothing personal is intended by our words or actions.

Having said that, let me assure you that our first desire is to work with you as fellow citizens, countrymen and public servants to achieve these goals. We greatly look forward to working with you as we endeavor to make Barry County a safer place to live for our families and friends.

 Best wishes and kind regards,

Skip Coryell
Director, SW Michigan
Ted Nugent United Sportsmen of America

I recall being surprised that they didn't respond to my letter. That was naïve of me. In retrospect, I've learned that people of unquestioned power do not easily surrender it. There is only one thing which people of power respond to: superior power. And there is only one thing that people of power want: more power. So, together (B-SAFR and TNUSA) threatened to sue the county for violating the Open Meetings Act, and within three months the county gun board meetings were moved to the courthouse and made open to the public. After that, we videotaped every meeting until our CCW bill was signed into law. In the end, words mean little, because words alone seldom get the job done. Words, backed up only by inaction and cowardice, will always ring empty and hollow. It is the words of a patriot, backed up by action and boldness, that will always win the day. I have learned that even the most powerful king can be deposed by the lowliest group of peasants if they possess sufficient courage and resilience. (Good timing and brains help too.)

Eventually, we got what we wanted. Not because we were smarter or stronger, but because we didn't quit. The passage of the Michigan shall-issue CCW law was a textbook example of "we the people" in action. Ordinary Americans united. We took names. We kicked ass. We took America back. Samuel Adams rolled over and smiled in his grave, and toasted to our boldness.

We've seen time and again how inalienable rights have been gradually eroded away like wind on rock, one grain at a time, until, they were gone. Ask our friends the Brits, the Canooks, and the Aussies. Most of their Second Amendment rights are now gone; only to return after decades of sweat or perhaps even the shedding of blood. What a shame. They are finding out, too late, that it's easier to defend that which you already have, than to regain that which you've lost.

In my second novel, the world's first geopolitical redneck thriller, titled "*We Hold These Truths*", I give a good example of grassroots activism. In this chapter, Lance Stuart is giving a speech at a local Second Amendment rally. But in real life, I had written this speech to commemorate Independence Day several years ago. I sent it in to Neal Dionne, who then read it on the air during his afternoon radio talk show on WOOD AM 1300 in Grand Rapids, Michigan. But I loved the speech so much, that I adapted it to be in my novel. It was a perfect fit.

I have included the speech below, and I hope that it inspires you to stand up and fight for your Second Amendment rights. Don't be a wimp! Stand up and fight!

"We hold these truths to be self-evident, that all men are created equal, that they are endowed by their creator with certain inalienable Rights, that among these are Life, Liberty, and the pursuit of Happiness."

I often wonder what Thomas Jefferson would say about the present course of human events if he were alive today. Would he be alarmed at the present trend towards liberalism and big-government control? Would Thomas Jefferson subscribe to the popular doctrine of political correctness, or would he rail against it? I think Thomas Jefferson would tilt his head to one side and ask, "What part of self-evident didn't you understand?"

The Declaration of Independence was based primarily on the Laws of Nature and of Nature's God. Laws of Nature, are intrinsically Laws of God, our Creator, higher laws, laws which when broken set off a chain of natural events and consequences which cannot be halted or harnessed regardless of what artificial law a man-made legislature may institute via a temporary government.

The Declaration of Independence, indeed our entire American

revolution, was a natural consequence of a government repeatedly breaking the laws of God and Nature. Many people today do not understand that the sole purpose of government is to protect these higher laws, and when government serves no longer as our protector, then they have become our oppressor and thereby a threat to our families and the liberty on which this great nation was founded.

"We hold these truths to be self-evident" Where did we lose our way, America? What part of self-evident don't we understand? How did the moral compass of our great nation become so skewed? We are indeed backwards: North has become South, and South has become North. The Bill of Rights was not written to protect government from the people, but rather, to protect the people from government, from the natural consequences of a corrupt government, wielding entirely too much power, in a way which perpetuates their downward spiral into graft and corruption.

There is a verse in the Bible which reads: "Woe to those who call evil good and good evil, who put darkness for light and light for darkness, who put bitter for sweet and sweet for bitter". How did we get here America? When did we turn our backs on the precepts and common sense on which this country was founded? As a country, we have collectively lost our way, and nothing short of a total about face can save us.

Our founding fathers recognized self-evident truth for what it was, and because of this, they pledged their lives, their fortunes, and their sacred honor. But with great Truth comes great responsibility, and our founding fathers were willing to die to preserve the natural laws of God and Nature. Indeed many of them made the supreme sacrifice for each and every one of us, and their blood cries out to us now from the ground they fought to free! Their blood cries out to every politically correct, brain-dead American who takes his freedom for granted, and who passively accepts without question the anti-American sentiment so prevalent in our society. Their blood cries out to us in outrage! "Did I die in vain! I gave my life, my fortune, my sacred honor so that you and your family could be free!"

"Whenever any form of government becomes destructive of these ends, it is the right of the people to alter or to abolish it!"

What part of this do we not understand? Our duty is clear. Parts of our government have become greedy, corrupt and repressive. "Destructive of these ends, ..." Our duty is clear! We must alter our government - now, while we still have the liberty to do so. We must get out and campaign and vote. We must write and talk and speak our minds! We must unite as Americans who love our country and are willing to work and live and die as did our forefathers. Now is the time to act! Do not be afraid of what people may think about you. Ours is not a spirit of fear, but a spirit of power! I implore you; I exhort you to press onward; to seize the day and all it holds while you still can!

Presently, there are those in our government who seek to strip away our rights and subjugate us one tiny piece at a time. But there is one right that we must not lose, because it is the gatekeeper of liberty. It is nothing more than the right to self defense; the right to hold our government accountable; a self-evident right, given to us by God. In short, the one right that protects all others. It is of course, the Second Amendment to the Constitution of the United States: the right to keep and bear arms. Our liberties, acknowledged by the Bill of Rights, stand side by side, lined up like dominoes, and when one falls, so do they all. And we are enslaved!

I urge you now, as we stand in the shadowy dusk of our independence, to remember and ponder the blood of our ancestors, the blood of those who fought and died so that we might live free. Do not cheapen its memory with apathy. Do not devalue its worth with passivity. Our founding fathers may have lived long ago, but there are natural powers which bind us together even beyond death, powers which transcend space and time, spiritual powers of the heart and soul of humanity. This bond cannot be denied or stripped from us. It is the irrevocable law of God and Nature. It is not a physical bond. It is a spiritual bond. A bond of the deepest, strongest kind - a bond of unseen blood!"

And in the immortal words of Forest Gump:
"I guess that's all I got to say about that."

"There are only two kinds of people that understand Marines: Marines and those who have met them in battle. Everyone else has a second-hand opinion."

— *Unknown* —

Never Give Up

Bite their Legs Off

On October 19th, 1950, over 120,000 screaming Chinese troops poured across the Yaloo River into North Korea. They attacked the 40,000 United Nations troops on all sides. Most of the UN troops were able to retreat south, but elements of the United States Marine Corps were trapped in the frozen Chosin Reservoir. For several weeks, the frostbitten and beleaguered Marines stood their ground, covering the retreat of the other UN forces, until they were ordered by General MacArthur to fight their way out.

It was during this battle, at an airstrip in Koto-ri, that the commanding officer of the 7th Marines, Lewis (Chesty) Puller was reputed to have summed up the situation like this:

> *"They're on our right; they're on our left; they're in front of us; they're behind us. They can't get away now!"*

I like that optimism. I can live with that. By the time it was all over, the Chinese had retaken North Korea, but it was at a tremendous price. In military terminology, the battle was classified as a "pyrrhic" victory for the Chinese.

The word *"pyrrhic"* originated from the Battle of Asculum in 279BC and in redneck terms simply means, "We won the battle, but most of us are dead." Thanks to the valiant stand of the 1st Marine

Division at Chosin, the victory for the Chinese was won at too high a cost, and they were forced to halt their advance. After the smoke cleared, 27,500 soldiers lay dead: 25,000 of them were Chinese.

What does this have to do with CCW holders? I spent six years in the Marine Corps, and that was enough to change me forever. Thank God they only had to change me once.

"Once a Marine, always a Marine!"

— Master Sergeant Paul Woyshner —

When I'm attacked, I don't retreat. I don't give up. I counter-attack! The best defense is a good offense. I guess I'm suffering from "Jarhead Syndrome": a terminal disease that leaves its victims stubborn, indomitable, and unyielding. When it comes to innocent civilians protecting themselves against bad guys, I wish we could all suffer from Jarhead Syndrome, at least until the fight is over and the criminal scum are hauled away on gurneys.

Florida recently passed the nation's first "Stand Your Ground" legislation. In simple terms, this means that we don't have to run from the bad guys anymore. We can stand our ground and fight to protect ourselves and our families. What kind of twisted, warped society mandates that its citizens must run from rapists, murderers, and thieves (i.e., the wretched refuse of the Earth) or face possible criminal and civil prosecution? Now I'm just a greasy, old, redneck, bowhunting, Marine, but that just "don't make no sense to me".

And I suspect that a lot of people are feeling the same way, because the "Stand Your Ground" legislation is sweeping the nation like a cleansing wave, washing away fear, and infusing Americans with courage and the will to fight back against rampant crime. Just as CCW shall-issue laws have taken over the country, so shall "Stand Your Ground". Most people don't want to be quivering cowards; that's not freedom! That's bondage! It's time for the criminals to fear and flee.

But the main point I want to get across in this chapter is this: "Once you decide to fight, you must do anything you can to win." Never give up, never give in, fight until the bad guy retreats or drops to the ground.

In my NRA classes, I'm not allowed to say "Shoot to kill!" But that's a political concern, brought about by the reality that there are lily-livered, soft-hearted, milk-toast wussies out there who would prefer that you die rather than defend yourself with deadly force.

Instead, we say: "Shoot to stop the threat." No matter what you call it, if you repeatedly double-tap the center of exposed mass I guarantee you the threat will stop. Bottom line is this: We stop the deadly threat by causing massive tissue damage and blood loss to our attacker. If they turn and run, great! It saves us all the price of expensive premium self defense ammo. If they choose to stand and fight, well, I can live with that too.

But once I decide to fight, my attitude has to be that of a United States Marine: "I will never lose. I will never retreat. I will win!"

I love the Marine Corps. They make me feel safe. And I especially love the way they speak their mind, despite the rash of political correctness infecting our nation. Because I am a Marine, I understand the way we think. But most people don't have that luxury.

"There are only two kinds of people that understand Marines: Marines and those who have met them in battle. Everyone else has a second-hand opinion."

— *Unknown* —

Make your attacker know you firsthand. Think like a Marine. Fight like a Marine. Never give up. Fight until one of you drops. Your family and all of society are depending on you.

The other day I was in a mood for a goofy movie, so I popped in "*Monty Python and the Holy Grail*". In the best comedy, there is always an element of truth. I was impressed by the Black Knight, who stood his ground and fought against King Arthur. A summary of the battle ensues below:

The brave and noble King Arthur comes to a bridge, which is defended by the Black Knight. He asks the Black Knight to join his court at Camelot and to help in his quest for the Holy Grail. The Black Knight turns him down, so King Arthur begins to move by on his way across the bridge. The Black Knight finally speaks.

"None shall pass!"

"What?"

"None shall pass!"

King Arthur tries to reason with him.

"I have no quarrel with you good Sir Knight, but I must cross this bridge."

"Then you shall die!"

King Arthur is surprised but quickly turns indignant.

"I command you as King of the Britons to stand aside!"

The Black Knight stands his ground.

"I move for no man!"

Resolved to cross the bridge, King Arthur and the Black Knight become locked in deadly sword-to-sword combat. But the king gains the advantage by cutting off the Black Knight's left arm. Blood gushes out for a moment, but quickly subsides. The king assumes victory, but the Black Knight refuses to yield.

"Tis but a scratch!"

"A scratch? Your arms off!"

"No it isn't!"

"Well, what's that then?"

"I've had worse."

"You lie."

"Come on you pansy!"

They continue to fight until the king hacks off the knight's other arm. The king assumes victory again, but the knight begins kicking him for all he's worth. King Arthur tries to convince him to stop, but the knight refuses to give up.

"It's just a flesh wound", he says.

The king is forced to cut off the Black Knight's right leg. The knight, undeterred, continues to hop on one leg and come at the king with head butts.

"Come here!"

"What are you going to do? Bleed on me?"

The knight replies.

"I'm invincible!

The left leg is hacked off and the Black Knight's torso and head plop onto the ground. The Black Knight looks up and says.

"All right. We'll call it a draw."

The king rides away with his servant as the Black Knight screams after him.

"Oh, I see. Running away? Come back here and take what's coming to you! I'll bite your legs off!"

So I say to all of you, never give up. Your attitude must be that of Major General Oliver P. Smith, USMC, Korea, December 1950.

"Retreat Hell! We're just attacking in another direction!"

It has been said that attitude is 90 percent of everything in life. I think it's closer to 95. I'm not saying to be stupid, like the Black Knight. I'm saying be brave. Bravery is not the absence of fear, it is the presence of courage in the face of danger.

Choose your battles wisely, but once you choose, never give up. There's no future in capitulation. Bite their legs off! Win!

A friend of mine came to me, one of my long-time Second Amendment activist buddies, and told me that he was going to walk through downtown main street openly carrying his pistol, daring the Chief of Police to arrest him. My first thought was: this doesn't sound like a good idea.

Open Carry Vs Concealed

Open Carry – Is America Ready?

Three years ago I wrote the following in the last version of my book *Blood in the Streets: Concealed Carry and the OK Corra*l:

"I teach my students that there is no advantage to anyone knowing that they are carrying a concealed pistol."

And then later on in the book I said:

"In my very humble opinion, in most scenarios, open carry is a bad decision. Open carry is stupid carry. Concealed carry is smart carry. Keep it hidden. Keep it smart."

For the past 8 years I have consistently taught in my classes that open carry is a very risky proposition, but I am starting to re-evaluate the severity of that opinion. I am always gathering new data, new experiences and new technology and then applying it to my everyday life. I think this is the best way to go, and I'm not so dogmatic as to think that nothing ever changes. Some things change, some things don't.

In my book I describe two reasons why open carry is stupid carry.

1. There is no tactical advantage to open carry.
2. It scares people. Michigan is not ready for open carry.

I believe that the first reason is open to debate and probably always will be. Open carry gives away the element of surprise and many people don't want to do that. Here's what I wrote in the first edition of the book.

> "As a former Marine Infantryman, I understand that the most important asset in a battle is the element of surprise. I know full well that if I can retain that equalizing "surprise element", then I can overcome most other odds, be they superior firepower or superior numbers. If I open carry, that advantage is gone. But if I carry concealed, I have a greater number of options that are open to me. I can wait and see what happens. I can duck behind cover. I can draw my firearm and surprise the bad guys with a hail of deadly gunfire. I can wait for them to make a mistake, then act decisively and with conviction."

However, despite all that, something happened last year which has caused me to re-evaluate my strong stance against open carry. Let me tell you what happened.

A friend of mine came to me, one of my long-time Second Amendment activist buddies, and told me that he was going to walk through downtown main street openly carrying his pistol, daring the Chief of Police to arrest him. My first thought was: this doesn't sound like a good idea. In fact, several years ago I had spoken with the Chief in that town and I knew that he was dead-set against open carry and even against concealed carry. Once, in a private conversation in his office, I asked him what he would do if I were to walk through town wearing a pistol and holster. He told me in no uncertain terms that he would arrest me. I believed him.

So when my friend came to me, I was concerned about his plan. I was convinced that he would be arrested. But then he asked me to join him and I didn't have the heart to tell him no. He was too good a friend and we'd been through the political activist trenches during the concealed carry debate, so we started making plans for the event.

Now you have to understand that I seldom do things small. It's just not in my personality. Besides, if I was going to walk through a city with a pistol strapped to my side, I wanted company. So I told a few friends, and they told their friends and then their friends told their friends – and then it hit the internet – all over the country. When I told Ted Nugent he was all for it and said to put it on tednugent.com, which I did. From there it migrated to other websites and soon I was getting emails from people all across the country.

This two-man event was growing out of control. And then the media started to call.

I figured since I was going to be interviewed by channel 3, channel 8, and the Detroit Free Press, that I might want to know something about open carry before I actually did it. So I emailed the guys at www.opencarry.org and they were very helpful, pointing me to videos of previous open carry events and other news sources. But I have to tell you, that even after I'd educated myself, I was still as nervous as a frog in a blender.

Just to be safe, we contacted the County Prosecutor, the State Police and the State Attorney General, just to make sure that what we were doing was legal. To my surprise, they all agreed that it was. They even pointed me to several legal sources: Attorney General Opinion 7101 on brandishing, and MCL 750.234d. I was reassured, but still nervous. Just to make sure, we recruited an attorney to attend our event, just in case.

All this happened in the span of four days, and on the night before, I didn't get to sleep until 4:30 AM. I emailed Ted Nugent for moral support and asked his advice. He emailed back in typical Tedlike fashion:

"YOU are in charge!! Carry on! Sincerity delivers the day. Godspeed"

Quite frankly, that's what he always says. Be sincere! Speak from the heart! Take control! He's such an alpha male. I secretly wished that he could fly on up and walk with me on this thing, but he had some lame excuse about a concert tour in Canada.

So I went to the event the next day with my wife and three kids. On the way there I called Dave and asked him how many people had come. He said he was still there alone. That was less than a half hour before the event. It was then I began to curse myself for being stupid enough to think that others would put themselves at risk alongside me. To top it all off, the kids were fighting with each other in the car and my nerves were tighter than a gnat's butt stretched over a barrel.

We got there and I saw TV cameras out front. I kicked into public relations activist overdrive and gave three interviews before even entering the building. When I got inside I was shocked to see the room was packed with about 50 Second Amendment supporters. Some of them I knew, others I didn't. But it was good to see them all. They were my backup.

I talked to the troops, telling them to keep smiling, say good things, and to not touch their firearms no matter what. Number one rule: 1. Pistols never clear leather. Number two rule: 2. Be nice, smile, live the golden rule.

Larry came up and told me that there was a group of anti's who might give us trouble. I thought to myself, *Great! Just what we need. Idiots bent on making us look bad!* I told everyone not to talk to them, just let them make fools of themselves. Any altercation would undoubtedly be blamed on us and defeat our mission which was to educate the public that open carry was both legal and constitutional and that gun owners need not be feared by the general population.

We walked outside, the cameras following our every move. We

walked down 2 blocks to city hall. Shopkeepers came out of their stores to watch, and people on the street took pictures with their cell phones.

A strange thing happened to me. I was no longer nervous. In fact, I was downright happy, gleeful even. It felt good to no longer have to hide my pistol behind a shirt. At that moment, while walking down main street with all eyes watching, I felt more like a free man than at any other point in my life.

We walked two blocks back to the county courthouse and gathered at the veteran's memorial in front of the fountain. I told them the story of how Dave and I had crashed our first County Gun Board meeting back in 1999, subsequently opening it up to the public. Then I gave a 5-minute speech. The Detroit Free Press called it a red-meat speech, but I'm not even sure what that means. Here's a small excerpt:

"We have been given a birthright of freedom, and that birthright was passed on to each one of us from our father and our father's father and his father before him. The right to keep and bear arms, the right to protect our families, the right to ward off the wolves is as old as creation itself. It was infused into our spiritual DNA, into the everlasting consciousness of humanity and it forever runs deep in the race."

I like red meat. Afterwards, people lingered, not wanting the moment to end. An hour later people were still there. Finally, I left, totally exhausted and my spirit fulfilled.

What we had done was risky, but the risk had paid off. Barry County was now open to "open carry". I'm glad we did it.

So, I find myself re-evaluating my stance. Obviously, many people still believe that concealed carry is the best tactical choice. Nonetheless, I suspect that many in America are ready for more. I believe that open carry, when properly practiced, is a useful tool in educating and desensitizing the public to firearm usage. For decades the anti's have taught that Guns equal crime; therefore, gun owners equal criminals.

That couldn't be further from the truth, and last week in a small town in Michigan, 40 plus gun owners proved it.

What I believe now

I hate the taste of crow. Even with garlic, butter and a few choice herbs and spices; it still doesn't taste like chicken. But on this one topic, I ate some crow, a full helping and then went back for seconds. I hope I never have to eat it again.

I had always been adamantly opposed to open carry, but something happened in my life that questioned my view. I was forced to re-evaluate and then to modify my position. It seems that all of life is a journey of adaptation and change. Some things change some things don't. The trick is to know the difference between the two.

I was able to meet a lot of good patriots because of this open carry venture: people like Brian Jeffs, Coordinator of Michigan Open Carry and John Pierce the co-founder of www.opencarry.org. Regardless of the tactical argument against open carry, I firmly believe that carrying a firearm is a choice and whether you openly display it or conceal it is none of my business. It's your constitutional right whether hidden or revealed, so wear your gun with pride! Personally, I prefer to carry concealed in urban environments just because I don't want to bring attention to myself. But when I'm out in the country pumping gas, mowing the lawn or walking in the woods, I just don't want to be bothered with extra clothing. I believe that your choice of carry method is just that - your choice, and no one should ridicule or judge you for it.

A word of caution

Open carry is legal in 44 of 50 states, so be sure to check it out before carrying in the open. The best source of information is the national website www.opencarry.org. I recommend you check it out, talk to the people there, and study up before jumping in.

Our society puts a stigma on guns that really shouldn't be there. It's not good for kids to view guns as a naughty and forbidden object, because human nature will drive them to it, like a moth drawn to the flame.

Children, Parents, and Guns

To listen to the anti-gunners talk, you'd think that half of all children born are accidentally shot to death by their parent's firearms. This couldn't be further from the truth. To the contrary, the vast majority of all firearm owners are responsible, safe, and ethical in every aspect of firearm ownership. But you've heard the old saying: "There's always that ten percent." So I'm writing this chapter primarily to those few morons who just don't get it, in hopes of reducing their numbers.

That last sentence reminds me of a story I read in the "Darwin Awards" a few years back. I believe they now have this story listed as an urban legend, but it's still a great story. If you're not familiar with this award, you should go to www.darwinawards.com, and read them every year just to remind yourself of the price of being stupid. On their website, the award is defined like this:

"The Darwin Awards salute the improvement of the human genome by honoring those who remove themselves from it in really stupid ways."

Or, more succinctly put, "Good riddance to bad rubbish!" The story that comes to mind went something like this:

Two rednecks were coming home from a frog hunt. And I use

the term redneck with all the affection one has for roadkill on a hot, sunny day. After all, I "are" one. (Redneck, not roadkill.) Where was I? Oh yes: "Rednecks on parade."

Two rednecks were coming home from a frog gigging expedition (only us rednecks will know what that means) when a fuse burned out in their truck, causing the lights to go out.

A replacement fuse was not available, but one of them noticed that the .22 caliber bullet from his pistol fit perfectly into the fuse box next to the steering wheel column. Upon inserting the bullet, the headlights again began to operate properly and they were on their way again.

After traveling approximately 20 miles, the bullet apparently overheated, discharged and struck one of the men in the right testicle. The vehicle swerved sharply to the right, exiting the pavement and striking a tree. The first man suffered only minor cuts and abrasions from the accident but required surgery to repair the other wound. The second man sustained a broken clavicle and was treated and released.

Now that's an interesting story on the human condition. So you're asking: "What does this have to do with children and guns?" Not a thing! But it sure was funny, so I wanted to pass it along. Laughter is medicine for the soul. Reminds me of Jeff Foxworthy: "You might be a redneck if . . . there's a hole in your right testicle." Just kidding, but I've always believed that in every legend there's an element of truth. As such, there's probably a man down South, perhaps in Arkansas, who still favors his right leg.

Now back to children and guns. Let's get serious now. In my NRA classes, I teach my students to keep all firearms out of unauthorized hands. And unauthorized is defined as anyone you decide should not have access to your firearms. Some on the list are cut and dried: small children, burglars, your mother-in-law, etc. I'm sorry. Did I say that last one out loud? Serious. Yes, I can do it! (Actually, my mother-in-law is a real sweetheart, but I couldn't resist the joke.) But let me remind you that we all live and die based on the decisions we make. So be careful when you make out your list. If it's too short, people who would otherwise protect you will be unable to do so. If it's too long? Well, let's just say that accidents can and do happen. Be careful.

For myself, I stay on the conservative side. There are only three people who can open my gun safe: myself, my wife, and my 20-year-old son. Everyone else is verboten.

My son and daughter are nine and eleven years old, respectively. My daughter, I trust implicitly around firearms. Not so with my son. To quote an old - but revered - comedian Red Skelton, "I wouldn't touch that line with a ten-foot pole!" Well, when it comes to my darling son, barring my direct supervision, I wouldn't let my beloved Phillip touch a gun with a ten-foot pole! Two kids, two distinct personalities and abilities. You have to take the time to get to know your kids so you can keep them safe from themselves. So much of being a responsible gun owner is just learning to be a responsible parent. That's not to say that my son never shoots a gun, because he does. He has a beebee gun and a .22 caliber rifle. But I keep them locked up, and he doesn't touch them when I'm not right there to supervise.

Our society puts a stigma on guns that really shouldn't be there. It's not good for kids to view guns as a naughty and forbidden object, because human nature will drive them to it, like a moth drawn to the flame. Kids are like that – people are like that!

With my children, they may touch any of my firearms, whenever they choose, under controlled conditions. First I unload it, then dismantle it, showing them how to clean it. I even let them help. They can touch all the parts, even reassemble it if they want, as long as I'm right there with them. When we're done, and their natural curiosity is satisfied, then it goes back inside the safe, and my kids go back to watching Veggie Tales. Curiosity may have killed the cat, but it doesn't have to kill our children. Take away the stigma or you'll transform your gun safe into Pandora's box, and, eventually, a resilient, smart child will find a way to open it up.

Now when it comes to smaller children, like toddlers, I take a different approach. They never touch my guns. They're just not old enough to understand the danger. Here's the approach I take with toddlers.

Have you ever heard the saying: "Childproof your home?" Well, I don't believe in that. In fact, I believe that in many cases it can lead to unnecessary injury and perhaps even death to an innocent child. You can childproof your home all you want, but once you leave the house, that child is once again in danger. Wouldn't it be smarter to "Homeproof your child"?

A long time ago, I read a book on Mennonite discipline, and, even though I'm not a Mennonite, I've incorporated what I learned into raising my own children. Mennonites "homeproof" their children like this:

When the child is approximately one year of age, they place the child on their lap, facing outward. Then they place a forbidden object in front of the child, within arm's reach. As soon as the child reaches for it, they slap him lightly on the hand and say "No!". The child pulls back. They do this for 15 minutes a day, gradually going through every forbidden object in the house, until the child knows what he can touch and what he cannot.

What does this teach your child? Boundaries, respect for authority, and accountability.

Note to parents: Don't try this with your teenagers; it won't work. I've tried it and you won't like it. But wouldn't it be nice if all teenagers were like this? Now I'm living in a dream world. Basic rule of thumb is: if they don't behave by time they're 10, you've got an uphill battle. Give yourself a break and catch them when they're young.

But just in case there are any future Darwin Award recipients reading this chapter, allow me to clarify: I still lock up my guns. I still put those little plastic covers on my electric outlets. I don't leave the Skil saw plugged in.

I home proof my child so that he doesn't kill himself. You can child proof your home, but that becomes meaningless when you visit friends without children. Katie bar the door and it's every man for himself, because the house is trashed! Breaking glass, chewed up knives, giant boogers in the microwave, dogs and cats sleeping together! It's total bedlam! And all because you didn't properly train your children.

When it comes specifically to guns as a forbidden object, I think the NRA's Eddie Eagle program is right on track. They take children and guns and boil it down to its most logical essence: "Stop! Don't touch! Leave the area! Tell an adult!"

My children have it memorized, and I quiz them on it often. Why is it necessary? Here's a case in point:

A friend of mine is a serious hunter as well as an avid gun collector. His house is both a museum and an arsenal. It has a nice ambience, and just thinking about it brings chills to my redneck, gun-totin' body. I love it! But here's one thing I don't love. He leaves some of those guns lying around the house loaded and leaning up against walls. That's an accident waiting to happen, and I've asked him to stop, but to no avail. Thankfully, my children have never touched any of them. They are prepared. I quiz/innoculate them like this:

Once a month, I take my pistol out of its holster, unload it, double-check it, lock open the slide; then I lay it down on the dining room table. I then walk over to the kitchen and clean or make dinner. I wait until my kids notice it, then I watch them. Every time - without exception - they have run up to me and scolded, "Daddy! You left your gun on the table again!"

I say, "Thank you, Sweetheart." Then I walk over and put it back in my holster where it belongs, feeling safe and assured that my kids will do the right thing when I'm not around.

Now, do I believe guns should be in schools? Of course I do! No thinking American would propose otherwise. Every teacher and principal who can safely and effectively use a firearm should be carrying in our schools. As Rush Limbaugh would facetiously say: "It's for the chirldens."

You and I have charged the schools to keep our children safe and to teach them. One gun in the wrong hands can levy a multitude of evil upon innocent children. Conversely, one gun in the hands of a safe, responsible parent, teacher, or principal can literally save the lives of the ones least able to defend themselves. But I'll argue that point further in a later chapter.

For now, let's just all try to get the NRA Eddie Eagle Gun Safety program into the elementary schools. Then we can get NRA marksmanship programs into high schools to teach them discipline and responsibility. I like that. It has a nice ring to it. Happy guns in happy schools! A safe gun, is a happy gun! Let's all smile now as we reload and double-tap dead-center of exposed "bad-guy" mass.

Blood in the Streets

100 yards down the road, the van skidded to a stop, turning sideways in the road, effectively blocking my path. I slowed to 20 miles per hour to give myself time to think. My pulse shot back up again. My hand was still held down steadily on the car horn, and my emergency flashers were still on. But there was no one around. I was on my own for this one.

Gutless, Yellow, Pie Slinger!

I teach my students that once they strap on a firearm, they will never be able to fight again. That probably seems odd to you, so let me elaborate.

When you carry a firearm for protection, you are also putting yourself in a potentially precarious position. As all police officers know, things have a way of escalating and getting out of hand. Any of you who have been through a nasty domestic experience or divorce also know that "things sometimes get out of control". As William Butler Yeats, the famous Irish poet once said in his poem: "The Second Coming"

> *"Turning and turning in the widening gyre*
> *The falcon cannot hear the falconer;*
> *Things fall apart; the center cannot hold;*
> *Mere anarchy is loosed upon the world."*

That phrase, "The Center cannot hold." Is crux and core to all of human existence. Things just have a way of breaking down: washing machines, cars, houses, relationships, etc.; they all fall apart, if not given constant attention.

When carrying a pistol, you must assume that every time you interact with another person there is potential for deadly conflict.

Let me give you some good advice: Never argue. Never altercate. Never insult.

There is no good that can come from it. Treat everyone you meet with the utmost dignity and respect, and most of your problems will be avoided. As always, the golden rule comes into play: "Do unto others, as you would have others do unto you."

I remember once, as a boy of 14, I was being bullied at school. I was looking for a way to protect myself. So I asked one of my neighbors, an adult I respected, this question:

"What is the best form of self defense?"

His answer was immediate and unflinching:

"A kind word."

I was very unhappy with that answer, so I disregarded his wisdom. Besides, I was fourteen. What did he know? He was just an adult anyway! Many times since then I have looked back and wished I had taken the man more seriously. It was some of the best advice I ever ignored.

Since then, I have been in many arguments, fights, altercations, and disagreements. Call them what you want, but none of them were fun and no good ever came from them. In almost every case I should have just walked away.

I remember several years ago, I was on my way into work at 4AM on a Saturday. The streets were deserted, and I was enjoying the solitude. I like thinking alone in my car. At the time, I was a single father, with custody of two children, and I valued my peace and quiet, though serenity was rare for me.

But my peaceful introspection was not to last. About 5 miles from work, a white panel van came out of nowhere and got right up on my bumper and began to tailgate me, all the while flashing his lights and honking his horn.

My first thought was: "Hmm, there must be something wrong with my car." But I checked my gages, and they were fine. The car was driving well. There was no smoke, no odd sounds, no vibrations. I almost pulled over, but something inside prevented me. It just didn't feel right.

At that point, the van pulled up in the left lane beside me. The driver rolled down his electric window on the passenger side and began cursing at the top of his voice. There seemed to be no one else with him, but I couldn't see in the back. I made a quick determination not to pull over, no matter what he did. Instead, I put on my emergency flashers, maintained a steady speed of 45 miles per hour and pressed down nonstop on my horn, trying to get someone else's attention.

I had no cell phone, and the streets were deserted. By now, my heart rate had increased, so I made a conscious effort to slow my breathing and my pulse. This helped some. I pulled my shirt up on my right side to gain easy access to my .40 caliber pistol, but I didn't touch it or reveal it to him.

After about ten seconds of honking and swearing, the man sped off. I was immediately relieved. My quick thinking had averted a potential crisis with a lunatic. But wait, 100 yards down the road, the van skidded to a stop, turning sideways in the road, effectively blocking my path. I slowed to 20 miles per hour to give myself time to think. My pulse shot back up again. My hand was still held down steadily on the car horn, and my emergency flashers were still on. But there was no one around. I was on my own for this one.

As I approached the van, I saw the man get out and walk around the back to place himself between myself and his vehicle. I had two seconds to decide what to do.

I slowed down a little bit more, then as I approached the van, I drove off the road, into the ditch, and around his vehicle. When I got back on the road, I accelerated to 45 miles per hour again. I glanced back in my rear-view mirror and saw the man run around to the driver's side and get back in the van. He laid a patch of rubber, and within a few seconds was back, just a few feet from my bumper.

He honked his horn again and continued flashing his lights. I stayed the course. A few seconds later, he pulled up beside me and continued to insult me with profanity in a very loud voice. I watched him as best I could while driving, just to make sure that no weapon was introduced. At this point, I was fearful but cognizant, and prepared for the possible use of deadly force. I struggled to control my breathing and lower my pulse rate throughout the entire altercation.

The man stayed another 10 seconds or so, then he sped away and I never saw him again. I drove on into work, a bit shaken, but alive, and my life went on as it had before the incident.

But I can't help but wonder: What would have happened if I had pulled over? What if I had responded with anger instead of alertness? How many were in the van? Did he have a weapon? Why was he doing this?

I will never know the answers to those questions. But at least I'm still alive to ponder them. I'm convinced that pulling over would have been the worst-possible plan of action. As it was, I drove away and carried on with my life. But if I had pulled over, the situation would have escalated. Yeats is right. "Things fall apart. The center cannot hold!"

Best-case scenario: I would have killed that man. Worst-case scenario: he would have killed me. There was no good that could have come of it. That morning was a valuable lesson for me. Up until then, teaching NRA Personal Protection classes was just all theory and book learning, but that altercation enhanced my teaching, giving it flesh and blood and bone.

I don't get into fights. I don't argue. I don't gesture disparagingly, and I don't antagonize or challenge unnecessarily. I avoid places where conflict is likely. I avoid crazy people. In my experience, when you let crazy people into your life, your life becomes crazy. I have no use for crazy.

When someone insults me, I try to smile. A smile is confident and disarming. If I can say something witty to diffuse the situation, then I do so. If I can't think of anything good to say, then I keep my mouth shut and walk away. It goes like this.

"Hey, you ugly jerk!"

"Have a nice day, sir."

I keep walking. Always keep walking. It may not seem like the most masculine or honorable thing to do, but it is the smartest response. It will save you thousands in legal fees, possible death or injury, and your life will go on undisturbed. If you stop, the situation will escalate, and no good will come of it.

I'm reminded of Marty McFly in "Back to the Future III". The town bully and gunslinger Buford "Mad Dog" Tannen, has just counted to ten and challenged Marty to a gun fight.

"Ten! Did you hear me, runt? I said, that's ten, you gutless, yellow pie slinger!"

Marty looks around the saloon at all the people staring at him, pressuring him to walk outside the saloon and die.

"He's an asshole! I don't care what Tannen says! And I don't care what anybody else says either!"

Marty McFly finally figured it out and so can you. Don't fight. Don't argue. Don't insult. Just walk away.

"Why should the law prevent us from protecting ourselves in our day care centers, our schools, our churches, and our sports arenas?"
　　— Alan Cropsey, Michigan Senator and MCRGO Board of Directors —

Pistol-free Insanity

On April 20th, 1999, Eric Harris and Dylan Klebold walked into the cafeteria at Columbine high school, at approximately 11:19AM. Another student heard Eric Harris yell "Go! Go!"

According to transcripts, a call was received by the 911 operator at exactly 11:25:05 AM. Six precious minutes had already passed, and innocent students were already bleeding and dying.

According to most timelines, the two boys were free to wander the school until 12:20 PM when they shot themselves. For over an hour, two crazy students, armed to the teeth, went from room to room, peering under tables and desks, looking for victims. And when they found someone, they simply shot them in cold blood – with impunity. They were very casual, unrushed, never worried about resistance, they simply killed as many as they could in the hour they had.

In all, Eric Harris and Dylan Klebold fired 188 shots, including 37 shotgun rounds and 151 9mm rounds, killing one teacher, 12 innocent students, and injuring 23 others. How did they do that? Why did no one stop them? How did they kill so many people?

The answer is: "easy". It was like shooting fish in a barrel, sheep in a pen; the students, faculty, and staff didn't fight back; they were unarmed, both physically and mentally. They hid beneath desks, waiting for the police to come and rescue them. It didn't happen. They died. Society's promise had failed them. The promise of gun control was a lie. At this point, I'll repeat the wisdom of Ted Nugent.

"Let me get this straight: Running, crying, whimpering, and hiding under desks and pews? You mean to say that when an imbecile walks into a church, office, a day care center, or school, stumbling about, almost zombie-like, with gun-filled hands at his side, blabbering incoherently to his next victim, the reaction of grown men and women is to run, cry, whimper, and hide under a desk or pew? The sheeping of America is nearly complete."

One marginal firearm in the hands of a teacher or administrator, even a janitor, could have saved many innocent lives, but it was not to be. Schools are a pistol-free zone, but, apparently, Dylan and Eric didn't get the memo. They broke a total of twenty-one federal, state, and local laws just to procure the firearms they used in the shootings, then untold more laws were broken when they entered school property and went on their shooting rampage.

It's almost as if – dare I say it - they didn't care about the law. Let's get down to basics for a minute:

Crim·i·nal – Noun – One who has committed a crime.

Those two boys became criminals when they broke their first law, which was long before they entered school property. Criminals, by nature and by definition, have no regard for the law. They only care about getting caught, hurt, or killed.

So, let's follow this definition to its inevitable conclusion using logic and "if-then" statements of fact.

If a criminal has no regard for the law, then, laws will not deter him. Kind of simple isn't it? Then why can't our legislators figure it out? Well, some can, but others can't. Our job as responsible citizens, is to vote out the ones who can't. In that regard, perhaps you and I also failed those students at Columbine. We allowed people with no common sense to lead us, and, like sheep, we followed blindly to witness their deaths.

And that's why I called this chapter "Pistol-free Insanity", because it makes no sense whatsoever to disarm honest, law-abiding citizens, potential "sheepdogs" who are willing to defend the flock from wolves. We do it over and over and over again. Someone is murdered, so we make a law against the way they did it. Someone else is murdered, so we make another law, and another and another, and another. Where does it end? Answer – never. Because that's how legislators gauge their success, by introducing bills and passing new laws. What we need is an anti-legislator, someone who will get rid of half the stupid laws we already have on the books. But I digress – again.

No doubt you've all heard this definition of the word, "insanity". "Doing the same thing over and over again, but, each time, expecting a different result." Gun control laws will never control criminals; they never have, and they never will. They only control those willing to obey, i.e., honest citizens.

So, even with the best of intentions, gun control laws are doomed from the start, because they are illogical and contrary to the laws of human nature. They affect only the victims of crime and leave the criminal unmolested, indeed, empowered to do his job quicker, easier, and safer.

But I say, "Make the criminal scum pay!" Armed sheep are a wolf's worst nightmare. Make the wolves worry. I want to see them twitch their head nervously from side to side when they mug someone. I want to see them develop nervous ticks! I want them scared. Loosen up gun laws and allow innocent victims to defend themselves. And that's what "shall issue" CCW laws and "stand your ground" bills are all about. Empower the people and let us take out the trash!

Am I advocating vigilantism? Of course not! That's against the law! However, when laws no longer serve the people, the people should work to abolish those laws. So, work hard to abolish counter-productive gun control laws, arm yourselves, train, stay alert, and, when the bad guy comes knockin', you start rockin'! It's the only thing that makes sense! Why? Because it works!

Aside from being illogical and impractical, pistol-free zones create unsafe conditions for all of society, for several reasons.

First and foremost, pistol-free zones create an artificial geo-graphical area where only criminals will have guns. You've seen the time-tested and popular bumper sticker: "Outlaw guns and only outlaws will have guns." This is very true. But, many of our legisla-tors, in their infinite stupidity, took it a step further. Not only did they create pistol-free zones, but they announced it to all criminals everywhere. "You may rape, pillage and plunder with impunity at the following locations: churches, schools, hospitals, casinos, daycare centers, and stadiums, etc." Someone emailed me a sign that would be funny if it weren't so scary. "Attention criminals! All law-abiding citizens have been disarmed in this location for your convenience."

Now tell me, does that make any sense to you? Where do peo-ple like Eric Harris and Dylan Klebold go when they want to kill mass amounts of people? The answer is obvious, they go to a place with lots of people, preferable unarmed people. Places like schools, churches, stadiums, . . . is any of this sinking in?

Think about this next question and take it to heart. If someone is already willing to commit mass murder, do you really think they care about a sign that says: "No guns allowed"? When did simple, common sense become so uncommon? It's amazing.

Here's another thing. As a former Marine and as an NRA Instructor, I've been around a lot of firearms in my day, so I know firsthand that guns don't pull their own triggers and bullets don't spontaneously combust inside the chamber. Someone has to pull the trigger or the blasted gun just won't go off! In short, guns don't go off inside the holster, they go off when they're being handled. And what do pistol-free zones mandate? They force CCW holders to continuously and needlessly handle their firearms, usually in a cramped and crowded place like a car. Allow me to illustrate by describing a typical day for many CCW holders.

7:45AM – Holster pistol and leave the house.

8AM: - Drop kids off at school. You have to go in and see the teacher, so you unholster your pistol and lock it in the car. You come back out, and reholster your pistol.

8:30AM - Go to the post office on your way to work. Remove gun. Put in safe. Go inside. Come back out. Handle gun again. Go to work.

9:00AM – Get to work. They are afraid of guns there, so you take it out and lock it up. (Handle it again.)

Noon: Go to lunch. (Chinese food) Take out gun, holster it. Return to work. Unholster gun.

5PM – Get off work. Holster gun.

5:45PM – Go get kids at daycare center. Unholster gun, put in gunsafe. Go in, get kids. Come out. Take gun out of safe and reholster it. Go home.

So, thanks to the pistol-free zones, instead of drawing my pistol once, I have handled my firearm a total of 11 times. Ten of those handlings were unnecessary, except for compliance with a ridiculous and senseless statute.

Why would the legislature do that? The answer is simple. It's called political compromise. In order to garner enough support to pass the bill into law, the bill was continually watered down to get moderates to vote for it. Plus the fact that anti-Second Amendment politicians don't want you carrying at all, so if they can't stop the law, they'll at least do their best to make it impractical to carry.

I find it an amazing tribute to God that he loves even anti-gun politicians. It's probably best that he's God and I'm not. But, alas, they are like the poor, they will always be with us. They are the wretched refuse, the scum of the earth, always seeking whom they may devour, constantly trying to entitle and enslave those without the guts to stand and fight against them. And that is the task of this generation, to stand and fight, to resist, to restore sanity to our legal system.

Now, with God as our witness, "Go forth and conquer!" Take no prisoners! Take America back, piece by piece if needs be, one pistol-free zone at a time!

> *"The price of freedom is eternal vigilance."*
> —*Thomas Jefferson*—

I was instructed to walk through the front door with my hands above my head. They had me back down the steps, then raise my shirt up to my armpits. It was dark outside and several very powerful lights were on me. One officer came out from behind cover and gave me a body search that was the envy of even the most overzealous Air Transportation Authority Agent.

Safety, Safety, Safety

Have you ever cussed at your computer? I have, many times. The problem with computers, is that they always do precisely what they're told to do, regardless of what you want them to do. In that regard, firearms are the same way. When I pull the trigger, the gun goes "bang". When I point the gun at a person, then pull the trigger, someone gets hurt or perhaps even dies. It's really quite simple.

So that begs the question, "If it's so simple, then why are there still gun accidents?" On page 211 of Ted Nugent's book "God, Guns, and Rock-n-roll" Ted makes this ingeniously basic assertion:

"And the bottom line remains that there is no such thing as an accidental discharge, only negligent discharges. It is never a hardware problem, always a human mistake. Period. So don't make the mistake."

And, of course, Ted is right. After all, he's Ted.

According to the NRA, rule number one of firearm safety is "Always keep the gun pointed in a safe direction". Rule number two is "Always keep your finger off the trigger until ready to shoot."

Rule number one is important, because "safe direction" is defined as any direction where the gun can discharge without hurting another person. Rule number two is important, because guns just don't go off unless someone pulls the trigger.

I suppose there are extremely rare exceptions to this rule, e.g., firearm malfunction of a very old gun that has been dropped, or, the spontaneous combustion of a CCW holder. But, for the most part, people and guns just don't burst into flames, and, if they do, you've got more to worry about than flying bullets.

I recall that when I took my NRA class to become a Basic Pistol Instructor, the teacher asked how many of us had ever had an accidental discharge. When 6 out of 7 of us raised their hands, I thought that there must be some mistake. Perhaps people misunderstood the question and thought he was asking about their sex life? After all, I was the only person in the room with no law enforcement experience. I was shocked to discover that every cop in the room had experienced the misfortune of having their gun go off by accident. How could that be? Police are highly trained.

Yes, of course they are. But if you think of a firearm as just another tool, then it becomes more clear. How many carpenters have you seen with missing fingers? It is so easy to become careless with a table saw when you operate it several hours a day. Likewise, when people are around guns everyday, they can become lax, they stop thinking, they make stupid mistakes, and they break the rules.

Life is cause and effect. If you neglect safety rules, the gun will go off and hurt or kill someone. In my instructor class, the teacher went around the room and made each of us tell the story of our "accidental" discharge. By time he got to me, I was sweating .45 caliber bullets. It's not a pretty story, but I'll tell it to you now. Go ahead and have a laugh at my expense, but it will be worth my embarrassment if you learn something that may save your life.

I grew up in the country around guns. I knew the rules. In fact, I had gone to great lengths to handle my firearm safely and to keep it out of unauthorized hands. Still, even with heightened awareness and after meticulous precautions, I screwed up.

I remember that I was about to file for divorce from my wife at the time. (Yes, this is a very juicy story. The soap operas have nothing on yours truly.) I had just caught her in her second affair, and I was holding off from filing, just to make extra sure I got custody of my two children. She was deep in the throes of drug and alcohol addiction, and I had been documenting everything. The pending court battle promised to be very nasty and I wanted to be prepared.

Bobby Napier, my hunting buddy, had come over to visit, and we were watching the movie "*Major Payne*" in the front living room. We were both sitting on the couch and my then-wife was off to one side in another chair. Halfway through the movie I said, "Hey, have I showed you my new .40 caliber yet?"

He said no, so I rushed off to the gun safe to get it. I brought the loaded gun into the living room, carefully removed the magazine and ejected the cartridge from the chamber. I double-checked to make sure it was safe before handing it to my buddy. I sat back down on the couch, put the magazine on my lap and went back to the movie as my friend looked over the gun and dry fired it a few times. When he was done, he handed the empty pistol back to me and I dry fired it a few times myself. I would pull up, aim at the television set, line up my sights, get good sight picture and sight alignment, then slowly and carefully pull the trigger rearward until it clicked. I did that several times over a 15-minute period, just for practice, then I stopped and placed the empty pistol on my lap.

About 10 minutes later, I grew tired of the loaded magazine sliding down into the couch cushions, so I slammed it back into the pistol and laid it back on my lap. A half hour later, I pulled up, aimed at Major Payne, and dry fired again. Wham! Major Payne exploded!

A .40 caliber inside a small room can make a deafening noise. I remember being totally shocked at the boom and at all the smoke.

I looked down at the gun in my quivering hands and thought. "Did that just go off?" The hole in my television set and the cloud of smoke above me confirmed that it had.

Bobby looked at me and said, "Are you mad at the TV or something?" I didn't answer. I was so shocked that I couldn't even speak.

My wife just stared over at me and smiled, very calmly and said, "Now I've got you."

I didn't know what she meant at the time, but after my buddy left a half hour later, she walked over to the phone and, with perfect poise, dialed 911. She then, very calmly, deliberately, and as if she'd been planning it for years, pretended to be terrified.

"Yes, hello, please! I need the police! My husband has a gun! He just shot the television and I'm scared. I have two small kids in the house and I don't know what he's going to do next!"

She had me by the balls, and I could feel the icy grip of her squeeze. I sat down across the room and listened as she spewed out lie after lie to the dispatcher. At one point I got up and walked over to take the phone, but she began screaming.

"Oh no! He's coming to get me!"

I wanted to strangle her. Instead, I prayed silently, and waited for the SWAT team to come and take me away.

Five minutes later, I was instructed to walk through the front door with my hands above my head. They had me back down the steps, then raise my shirt up to my armpits. It was dark outside and several very powerful lights were on me. One officer came out from behind cover and gave me a body search that was the envy of even the most overzealous Air Transportation Authority Agent.

The officers were very professional. They got my story. Then they got hers. Mine was consistent, but hers was not. Because the police were already familiar with our precarious marital situation and because they had arrested her before on other charges, they chose to believe my story, and they let me off with a warning to be more safe. I was lucky.

To make a long story short, I divorced her, got the house, the kids, child support, etc. But that one instance of stupid, mindless, neglect of firearm safety gave me fits in court for months to come. (Not to mention that I had to buy another television.)

What rule had I broken? A big one.

The NRA specifically teaches that no ammo is to be in the room while dry firing. Ouch! Almost a decade later, it still embarrasses me to tell that story. My kids love the movie "*Major Payne*", but I can't watch it anymore. Even the sight of Damon Wayans makes me nervous!

And that's why I'm such a gun-safety nut on and off the range. My own stupid carelessness scared me into being safe. In that regard, it was one of the best things that ever happened to me. After that, I took an NRA gun safety course, then a few years later became an NRA Instructor.

You might call me the Apostle Paul of gun safety.

Yes, I was the chiefest of firearm safety sinners, but that blinding flash of light coming from my .40 caliber that evening caused me to rethink and to change. It opened my eyes, and, just like Paul, I had become "born again".

So I urge all of you, to rethink your stance on firearm safety. Be conservative. Be careful. Always think, and always obey the rules. They will save your life.

Don't wait for the blinding flash to learn and practice gun safety. Because, after the flash, it's too late for everything except the chalkline.

I quickly unholstered, placed the barrel of my gun on his bicep and pulled the trigger.
The blast blew blood, muscle and bone up against my living room door. The grip of his hand loosened and then fell away completely as he withdrew and fled, leaving an awesome trail of blood.

Stay Alert - Stay Alive

Just a few moments ago, while I was writing this chapter, I heard the dogs barking, and my mind and senses kicked into super, self defense overdrive. I heard a knock at the door and got up to answer it. But, something didn't feel quite right, so I first peeked out the curtain to see who was on the front porch. It was a rough-looking stranger.

Through the door, I asked who it was. He replied that his car had broken down and his wife and kids were stranded just down the road. This had the look and feel of truth, but I still wasn't convinced. I placed my foot about six inches away from the door and reached back to place my hand on my pistol. Then I slowly unlocked and opened the door a few inches.

Almost immediately, the man threw his body against the door, but my foot stopped it from flying open all the way. I was off balance and a little surprised, but was still able to push against the door and try to lock it back up. But the man was strong and heavy. Quickly, he reached in and clasped his big, heavy hand firmly around my throat and began squeezing. My right hand was still on my pistol, so I quickly unholstered, placed the barrel of my gun on his bicep and pulled the trigger.

The blast blew blood, muscle and bone up against my living room door. The grip of his hand loosened and then fell away completely as he withdrew and fled, leaving an awesome trail of blood. I closed the door, locked it, and then called 911 as I went to check on my kids.

It's okay, relax, I didn't really shoot anybody. It was just a drill. In an earlier chapter, I mentioned a self defense training technique called visualization. I practice this technique everyday without fail. It's something that I do automatically, without even thinking about it. By now, it's become so ingrained in me, that I doubt I could stop if I tried. You can't just run out and buy yourself a gun and then expect to survive a gunfight. You have to prepare. You have to train.

> *"Owning a handgun doesn't make you armed,*
> *anymore than owning a guitar makes you a*
> *musician."*
> — *Jeff Cooper, Author of "Principles of Personal*
> *Defense" —*

Quite often, I'll be driving down the road, and my wife will see a very concerned look on my face. She'll say, "Honey, what are you thinking about? Is something wrong?" Usually, I'll respond something like this. "No, everything's fine. I was just imagining that we stopped to help someone hurt on the side of the road and they pulled a gun on me. It's okay. I killed them." She's a good woman, and she always reaches over and gives my arm a reassuring squeeze before saying "Thank you, sweetheart."

So, let there be no misunderstanding. When a man sticks a gun in my face, his life is forfeit. He has taken his own life. When a man tries to hurt my children, he'd better be wrapped in Kevlar, because

I'm going to come after him with everything I've got. If a man tries to rape my wife, his testicles will be hanging in my trophy room as soon as they return from the taxidermist. Now there's a vivid image.

Most often, when violent attacks occur, they happen quickly, without warning, and are extremely violent. FBI statistics tell us that the average firefight lasts 3 seconds, takes 3 shots, and occurs at a distance of 3 yards. That information tells us a lot, and helps us to properly train and prepare for survival of a violent attack

Retired Special Forces Colonel David Hackworth had a saying, which I always quote to my students: "Stay alert, stay alive." It's a code I live by. You would be well advised to do the same. I'm not saying that you should walk around paranoid and turn yourself into a nervous wreck. Let's be honest here. No one can be on full alert all the time. We would suffer from battle fatigue if we tried that. There's just too much stress involved in chronic, full-alert status.

But you can arrange your life in such a way as to enhance your chances of survival without adding stress to your life. I just read a very good article yesterday titled *"What Really Happens in a Gunfight"* written by Dave Spaulding. In the article, he talks about the almost 200 survivors of gunfights he has interviewed over the past 25 years. One common thing he discovered among those who won their gun battle was this: they were not caught off guard. They were able to quickly master and control their startle response. Many of them even recalled being angry instead of afraid and were able to channel the anger into useful energy.

But fear will push you to freeze. That's what startle response is, that initial 1 or 2 seconds at the beginning of a gunfight where the victim's body surges with adrenaline and he gets that "Oh my god I'm going to die" feeling in the pit of his stomach. It was also reported that those with less startle response were aware of their surroundings, and some had even practiced the technique of visualization.

There is a verse in the Bible which says that it is appointed unto a man once to live, and once to die. We all have that in common, and no man knows the day or season of his own death. I'm always amazed at the mindset of some people who try to tell me that I don't need a gun. Their lame argument goes something like this:

"You've never been attacked before, so you don't need a gun now. You're only going to get yourself into trouble. Just let the police protect you. That's what they're for."

Depending on my mood and my patience level, I'll respond in one of several ways. If I think they're trying to jerk my chain, then I'll just say "Opinions vary" and walk away, thereby diffusing the situation. But if I think they're serious and open to change, then I may say something like this:

"I heard your house burned down last week. Is that true?"

The look of surprise on their face is always priceless.

"No! Of course not! Who told you that?"

"Oh, I'm sorry. So when was it that your house burned down?"

"What are you talking about? My house has never burned down. Who told you that?"

"But you have fire insurance don't you?"

By now the man is getting impatient with me.

"Of course I do. What idiot would go without fire insurance?"

I respond calmly and matter of factly.

"The same idiot who walks around without the means to protect himself. My gun is my life insurance policy. I carry the policy because more people are victims of violent crimes than are victims of arson. I find it amazing that you spend thousands of dollars over your lifetime to insure something that can be replaced, but give no thought to your own life or the lives of your family who are priceless and irreplaceable."

Then I walk away. My point is made, and they have opportunity for rational thought. Ted Nugent once explained it to me this way in an email message:

"To be unarmed and therefore helpless in the face of evil is irresponsible and in fact complicit to said evil. If you knowingly and intentionally go forward incapable of stopping evil, you assist in its progress. A government that by law forces good people to be defenseless is in itself complicit to the recidivistic evil it helps create through plea bargaining, parole and early release policies! Only a person free to choose to protect himself is truly respecting God's gift of life.

— Ted Nugent —

I stay alert in every aspect of my life. I train, I prepare, I survive.

Yesterday, in the Advanced CCW class that I teach, one of my students was staring at me, hanging on every word. I thought it odd, because I was only a few minutes into the class. I was still trying to loosen things up and set people at ease. I looked at him and said: "You have a very serious look on your face. What are you thinking about?"

The floodgates opened and he spoke for ten minutes, telling the story of how his son-in-law had been brutally murdered the month before. The killing occurred in his own home, with a knife, and the murderer was the victim's own brother.

My student told the story of how he'd knocked on the front door of his son-in-law's house, hearing noises inside, but had been unable to enter through the locked door to investigate. Several hours later, he and his daughter, found the bloody remains of their loved one in the basement, brutally and savagely cut with a knife. The murdering brother turned himself in the next day, but that was no consolation to the wife and three children who were left behind. The murderer was a diagnosed paranoid schizophrenic who had stopped taking his medication.

The world is smaller than it used to be. We all live closer together, brushing elbows more often, getting on each other's nerves, causing confrontation to happen more and more. It is inevitable. When the pool gets crowded, people bump elbows.

Sometimes I wonder what has become of America. When I grew up, we didn't even lock our doors at night. Only a fool would do that now. I suspect that the breakdown of society was caused by a combination of many things. Our families are no longer healthy and intact. Blood, murder and violence on television has desensitized us to killing in general. The proliferation of online pornography has taught us that women are not people, but simply objects to be used for our own pleasure. The criminal justice system has become largely impotent and ineffective, allowing people to commit murder, almost with impunity. And last, but not least, moral relativism has permeated our society, telling us that there is no right and wrong, no good or bad, that each person must decide what is right in his own mind. (Of course, in the mind of a paranoid schizophrenic, the right thing to do is to kill your brother with a knife.) God, the ultimate authority on right and wrong, is being systematically removed from our schools, the courts, and from the legislative process.

As always, "cause and effect" reign supreme. Without God, there is no accountability and no ultimate punishment after death. The deterrence that once held the wolves at bay has been removed and it's "Katie bar the door".

Things aren't right with America or the world, and that's why I carry a gun; that's why I train; that's why I train others. The post-nine-eleven society of our beloved country is different than the land of our fathers. Sometimes it seems like the world has gone crazy. How shall we then live? How shall we then survive?

Some self defense instructors teach their students to think this way: "If you are attacked, then do this."

I teach my students: "*When* you are attacked, do this."

The difference is subtle, but very powerful. The word "*if*" implies that it may never happen, which is true. But the level of threat is so high, that you can't afford to take that attitude. The word "*when*" is more definite, and it puts you in a higher state of readiness. "When I am attacked, I will move to cover, draw my firearm and kill my attacker." That is definite. That is predictable. That is something you can train and be prepared for.

We can take America back, one life, one family, one community at a time. Start in your own house.

The wolf is at the door. When he comes in, blow his head off. He'll never hurt another little lamb.

Stay alert. Stay alive. Protect your family.

I remember the first time I used a public toilet while carrying concealed. I loosened my pants and the weight of my pistol sent them careening to the ceramic tile floor with a loud crack.

Packing Heat is a Pain

I remember the day I picked up my concealed pistol license from the County Clerk's office. It was more exciting than shooting an 8-point buck! I had worked hard, standing shoulder to shoulder alongside thousands of other citizen activists to obtain the legal status to that God-given right to keep and bear arms. So as soon as I got my permit, I drove home to get my pistol. It was then that I realized that I didn't own a holster. After all, I'd never needed one before. Not to be deterred, I shoved it into the waistband in the small of my back, put on a long shirt and went downtown. I must have walked up and down the sidewalk for an hour, going from store to store, reveling inside at my newfound right. I was 43 years old, but never in my lifetime had I been allowed by the government to carry a firearm for my own protection. I have always resented that about government.

But in retrospect, what is most interesting to me was the overwhelming feeling of guilt and fear I experienced. It stayed with me for several months until I realized that it was real, that the government wasn't going to arrest me for carrying a firearm. I look back on that time with a bit of sadness now. The very thought that I should be afraid of my elected officials and of law enforcement is sobering. But you'll read more about that in the next chapter.

That newfound excitement of carrying concealed lasted about 6 months, then it began to get old, as all routine things inevitably do. I quickly discovered that carrying concealed was a real pain in the butt. I opted to carry strong side with a belt slide holster on my right hip. It was comfortable and made my firearm quickly accessible. However, the drawback was that every once in a while someone would get a glimpse of my holster, either when the wind blew my jacket up or when I bent at the waist. It only happened a few times, but I quickly learned that it was not in my best interest for anyone to see me carrying a firearm.

So the quest for the perfect carry rig was on! I tried shoulder holsters, but my full framed .40 caliber wouldn't hide very well under my arm. The vertical rig dug into my armpit, and the horizontal holster jutted out so far to the front that I looked like I had a giant tumor growing on my chest.

I tried inside the waistband holsters, but quickly learned that I needed to buy all new pants, 4 inches bigger in the waist, in order to leave room for the pistol. For me, it was harder to draw the pistol, and it seemed uncomfortable as well.

I tried fanny packs, and they were fairly comfortable, allowing me to carry my cell phone and a spare magazine. I liked it, but people always thought I was gay. I don't like the idea of strapping a purse around my waist.

I tried a cross draw holster, ankle holster, even carrying in my pocket. However, at the end of the day, I was convinced that no single carry method is right for everyone. Eventually, I opted for a system of carry that incorporated several methods and holsters.

When I jog, I use a fanny pack. (I have a very masculine gait, so I guess it's okay.) When I want deep concealment, I'll go with an inside the waistband holster, no matter how uncomfortable it is or how tight my pants are.

For short distances, e.g., going from the car to the house, I may just tuck it into my waistband in the small of my back. I am amazed at how secure and comfortable that can be with a full-sized pistol. It's very easy to conceal, to draw, and never falls out on me. (Don't forget to wear a good belt.)

It seems that everything about concealed carry always ends up being a compromise. A larger caliber pistol is heavier, bulkier, harder to conceal, so you end up carrying a .40 caliber instead of that Desert Eagle you have so much confidence in. In the hot, summer months, concealability becomes an even greater concern. How can I stay cool and still carry the gun that gives me confidence. Well, sometimes I don't. Compromise is a way of life it seems.

There are a lot of things about concealed carry that surprise you when it first happens. I remember the first time I used a public toilet while carrying concealed. I loosened my pants and the weight of my pistol sent them careening to the ceramic tile floor with a loud crack. Fortunately, my pistol was undamaged, but I learned to slowly lower my pants down and gently lay them on the floor.

Since then, I've heard horror stories from people who lay their pistol behind them on the toilet tank before sitting down. Eventually, they walk off without their pistol. I imagine more than one person has watched helplessly as their five hundred dollar pistol slowly slid down into the toilet bowl. For a while, I took to laying my pistol on top of the toilet paper dispenser until one time the entire dispenser fell off the wall and my gun crashed to the floor.

Another problem is "huggers". No, that's not a typo. I said "huggers" not "muggers". This is always a problem at church. Some people are always coming up and giving me hugs, putting their arm around my waist and finding their hand touching something very large and hard. When I see the surprised look on their face, I just smile. One of these days I'm going to say "It's not a banana, I'm just very happy to see you." I think the older ladies, in particular, will appreciate that.

There are other problems too. My kids, while they like the idea that I carry a pistol and can protect them, they sometimes bump their head up against the grip of my pistol. I have learned to turn slightly when they approach for a hug so as not to hurt them. And, of course, whenever we wrestle and play I have to take it off and store it somewhere safe.

Sitting down is a pain. Getting in and out of the car is a pain. Going to the bathroom is a pain. So if carrying a pistol is such a pain, then why do I even bother? Sometimes I find myself tempted to leave the house without my pistol just to gain freedom from the bulk and weight. But I always resist that temptation. Carrying my pistol is tantamount to buckling my seat belt. I do both religiously, because someday they will save my life or the lives of someone I love.

In short, it's an inconvenience and it's a pain, but it's worth it. Besides, after all these years with a pistol strapped to my side, I would feel naked without it. It's a reassuring bulk that I never want to be without.

It's my life insurance policy, but it's only in force when I have it with me. It will take some doing, but if you work at it, you will find a carry system that works for you.

It's an inconvenience that you can live with.

"I just don't feel safe walking around anymore, especially when I'm in a big city. If they can take down the Twin Towers, then no one is safe."

CCW and Nine-eleven

There are certain days in your life that you will always remember, whether it be good, bad, pleasant or painful. Nine-eleven will always be one of those days for me. I remember that I was in Grand Rapids when I first learned of the Twin Towers tragedy. I had just pulled into work at Smiths Aerospace, and I was listening to B-93. Reese Rickards came over the air and told all of West Michigan about it, so I listened for a few minutes and then ran into work and looked on the internet for more information. My company set up televisions and most of us watched the news coverage all morning long. I remember vividly, watching real-time as the mammoth buildings crashed to the New York City pavement. That moment changed the world forever, and nothing will ever be the same.

It was very difficult for me to sit at my desk all that day, totally unarmed. Because of company policy, my pistol was locked in my car as it was every day at work. But on nine-eleven, it bothered me more than usual. Our country was under attack, and I was defenseless. I remember feeling especially vulnerable and impotent for months to come. Something deep inside me had changed and it took a long time for me to realize it, and then to get a handle on exactly what it was.

But one thing happened right away: attendance at my CCW classes skyrocketed. It was a bittersweet reality for me for several reasons. On the one hand, I was helping to train parents to defend their children, and that always made me feel good. On the other hand, I didn't like prospering monetarily because of an event that had cost so many innocent America lives.

Before each class, I always go around the room and ask each student several things: their name, where they live, their experience with firearms, and why they are taking the class. After nine-eleven, the reasons for taking my class changed for quite a few people. Here are just a few of the things they told me.

"I'm afraid now. I never used to be, but I am now."

"People out there want to kill us! I need to be able to protect myself and my family against those lunatics!"

"I don't feel safe walking around anymore, especially when I'm in a big city. If they can take out the Twin Towers, then no one is safe."

So I started holding classes every month, and attendance went from 5 to 10 students to 20 to 30 on average. Nine-eleven was the clarion call to all ostriches with their heads still in the sand. Wake up and smell the terrorists! They are here and they are not going away.

I was deeply affected by nine-eleven, so much so, that I felt compelled to write my second novel "*We Hold These Truths*". But before I could write it, I had to do a lot of research on radical Islam. I needed to understand why they wanted to kill innocent people. I read several books, two of them by Mark Gabriel, who was a former Professor of Islamic history at the Al-Azhar University in Cairo, Egypt. I found both his books "*Islam and Terrorism*" and "*Islam and the Jews*" to be especially enlightening. I found it amazing that on the day he told his father of his conversion to Christianity, his father pulled a pistol out of his belt and began shooting at him. Dr. Gabriel barely escaped Egypt with his life. Today, he lives in the United States, unable to safely return to his home country.

Another book I read, written by Steven Emerson, was titled *"American Jihad: The Terrorists Living Among Us"*. This book chronicles the rise of Islam in America and also details the recent history of terrorist groups around the world.

Last, but certainly not least, I solicited help from one of my closest friends as an Islamic Cultural Consultant. My friend, Phil Walsh, had roomed with me in college, and we had remained close friends to this day. Phil had grown up in the Moslem country of Bangladesh and was able to articulate quite clearly the mindset that drives radical Islam. Without the afore-mentioned books and Phil's expertise, I could never have written a realistic book on terrorism or created the antagonist character, Momin Islam, in my novel. I just didn't have the background for it.

The below excerpt from *"We Hold These Truths"* pretty much sums up how radical Islam views America. This scene takes place a day after the terrorist has just detonated a nuclear suitcase bomb on American soil. After that, he fled to Northern Michigan, where he killed a police officer. In this scene, he has been captured by three of the townspeople (two are CCW Instructors) and they are holding him captive in a church. FBI Special Agent Richard Resnik is explaining to them what radical Islam is really all about.

◆ ◆ ◆

"Make sure that duct tape is good and tight Zeke. Only God knows how many more of us will die if that lunatic gets away."

Zeke finished securing Momin's hands and feet and slowly backed away from the 8-feet tall wooden cross made of barn beams. They had placed Momin squarely in the center of the podium, to the left of the preacher's pulpit and to the right of the prayer candle display where they could watch him and still not have to get close.

Momin looked up at the cross and sneered.

"You can't stop me! Allah has willed it! You will all die in blood and fire!"

Zeke yelled back at him, more out of fear than anger.

"Just shut up! You're not going to kill anyone else ever again. If I had my way you'd be dead already!"

Momin laughed out loud.

"Then I will pray that you never get your way. You can't kill me until my destiny is complete. Allah will protect me until my work is done."

Josh took a step forward.

"How can you say that? You're a murderer – a mass murderer – you killed almost 200,000 people!"

Momin stopped laughing and his face became serious.

"Jihad is not murder. It is honor. It is duty to God."

Josh put his pistol back in its holster.

"That's the sickest thing I've ever heard! You call killing innocent women and children honor? What is honorable about that?"

Momin glared back at them, then turned his head and spit on the base of the large wooden cross.

"There are no innocents outside of Islam. This is Jihad. All must convert or be put to the sword!"

Lance Stuart had been quiet, but he stepped forward now, replacing his pistol in its holster as he did.

"I know that you believe that garbage and are willing to die for it, but why? How did you get so misled?"

The darkness of Momin's eyes looked up at him from ten feet away and glistened in the fluorescent light. When he spoke, it was in Arabic, and he went on for several sentences, spewing the words out like venom.

"He's speaking Arabic. Would you like me to interpret for you?"

Zeke, Josh, and Lance, all turned around and looked at

Richard Resnik, who had moved up to a sitting position on his cot. Josh walked over and sat beside him.

"You okay now agent Resnik?"

Richard smiled weakly and nodded.

"Yes. Just feeling very weak. And my fingers and toes are sore. They feel tender to the touch."

Zeke took a step closer.

"It's the frostbite. I saw a lot of it in Korea. A couple of your toes were black. You might lose one or two of them. But you'll be fine aside from that."

Richard looked up at the podium and met Momin's hateful gaze. He didn't flinch. This man had killed his family: his mother, his father, and 200,000 others.

"He was quoting from Osama Bin Laden who issued a fatwa against all Americans and Jews in 1998."

Zeke interrupted him.

"What's a fatwa? Never heard of it before."

"It's a religious ruling given by high-ranking Muslim leaders. This one was made public by the World Islamic Front in 1998 and supported by a great portion of the Muslim extremists."

Momin glared at him, his eyes full of hatred.

"Just shut up you stinking Jew! You are the first one I'm going to kill!"

Lance seemed to have adapted to Momin's fanatical spewings and just ignored him.

"What did the fatwa say?"

Richard stood weakly to his feet. Josh stood beside him, placing his hand on his back for support.

"Osama Bin Laden said: 'But when the forbidden months are past, then fight and slay the pagans wherever ye find them, seize them, beleaguer them, and lie in wait for them in every stratagem; and peace be upon our prophet Muhammad Bin-Abdullah, who said: I have been sent with the sword between my hands to ensure that no one but Allah is worshipped, Allah who put my livelihood under the shadow of my spear and who inflicts humiliation and scorn on those who disobey my orders."

Josh interrupted him.

"Slay the pagans? But we're not pagans. We're God-fearing Christians! We believe in God and we want to serve Him. America is still predominantly a godly country. So why are they killing us?"

Richard smiled weakly and shook his head from side to side.

"You don't understand radical Islam. It was founded by one man, a man with self-serving interests, and he spread his power and influence by conquering others. Muhammad claimed to be God's prophet, therefore, anything he said was considered equal to that of God. Did you know that Muhammad had 23 wives and concubines? Once he wanted to marry the wife of his step-son, something that was forbidden by Islamic law, so he simply claimed to have received a revelation from Allah that it was now lawful for him to take her as his wife. His step-son, who was a good Muslim, wanted to please the prophet, so he immediately divorced his wife so Muhammad could bed her. On another time, Muhammad, the great prophet of Allah, married a 6-year old girl, then consummated that marriage when she was only 9 years old. America must come to understand Islam for what it really is. Allah is not the god of Judaism and Christianity. He is not the god of love and tolerance."

Zeke turned away from Momin and faced Richard before the cot.

"I still don't understand why they want to kill us all. Even if all of that is true, it doesn't make any sense to me."

"It's because they define pagan as anyone who doesn't practice Islam. And, according to certain passages in the Koran, all pagans have to be converted or killed."

Richard looked down at the floor and thought for a moment.

He wanted them to understand what kind of person they had captured. He needed them to help him retrieve the other nuclear suitcase bomb and then take it back to the bureau.

"Later in the fatwa, Osama Bin Laden said: 'We – with Allah's help – call on every Muslim who believes in Allah and wishes to be rewarded to comply with Allah's order to kill the Americans and plunder their money wherever and whenever they can find it. We also call on Muslim ulema, leaders, youths, and soldiers to launch the raid on Satan's U.S. troops and the devil's supporters allying with them, and to displace those who are behind them so that they may learn a lesson.'"

Zeke, Josh, and Lance all stood motionless, saying nothing, surprised to learn that according to Islam, they were servants and soldiers of Satan. Momin saw the looks on their faces and laughed out loud maniacally.

"And now you know the truth! You are infidels, pagans, arrogant soldiers of the great Satan! And since you are soldiers, then you are enemies, and you must die. America and the weakness of Christianity has stood in Islam's way far too long. And now, you will be crushed under the iron boot of Islam. It is time for America to die!"

Zeke turned and yelled at the top of his voice.

"Just shut up! We don't want to hear your garbage anymore! America is free, and I fought to protect that freedom. I watched hundreds of my friends die trying to stop tyrants like you from enslaving other people."

"Hush Zeke!" Josh silenced him with a stern rebuke and a stare. "Don't lower yourself. He's not worth it. He's going to prison now, and he'll rot there for the rest of his life."

Momin smiled a tooth-filled grin.

"Go ahead and kill me! 70 virgins await me, and Allah will welcome me personally at the gates of Heaven."

Lance turned back around and glared at Momin.

"It's a good thing for you that we're in the house of God, because right now you are really getting on my nerves."

Josh walked up to the cross and looked down at Momin.

"Jesus commanded us to love you, so I can't go ahead and kill you, even though right now my fallen flesh wants ...."

Josh let the sentence die unended. He walked over to Momin, picked up the duct tape and wrapped it around his head several times, securely covering his mouth. When he was done, he nodded his head in satisfaction.

"There! You're easier to love when you're not talking."

I know that the above chapter probably sounds harsh and unpalatable to most Americans, but it really is an accurate picture of an Islamic terrorist. Most terrorists are raised in a third-world country where human life has lesser value. People die from disease, starvation, and murder everyday. Those who live, are destined to spend a lifetime in poverty and squalor. To someone such as this, the promise of seventy virgins and an elevated position in Heaven is very appealing. I often wondered why suicide bombers were so willing to blow themselves up, and I learned that there is only one way for a Moslem to guarantee his entrance into Heaven, and that is to die in Jihad. In conditions such as this, radical Islam flourishes.

I believe that it is only a matter of time before another attack occurs on American soil. The terrorists will not stop until one of two things occur: 1) They succeed in killing or converting all infidels, or, 2) They are stopped and contained using superior force.

Only one nation is capable of doing that – America – and that is why they hate us. We are a threat and an obstacle to them. Ever since nine-eleven, I have believed that we are fighting the battles of World War III, but most people don't understand that. That is due, in part, to the selective reporting of the mainstream press, and also because of the unconventionality of the nature of this war. There are no fronts, no battle lines, no uniforms, and no civilians. According to Islamic terrorists, there are only Muslims on the one hand, and infidels who must turn or be put to the sword on the other.

Have you ever noticed that after the first week of nine-eleven, the footage of the Twin Towers falling is rarely, if ever, shown? I believe that it is a dangerous thing to forget the past. The Twin Towers falling is the reason we fight. On the cover of my novel you'll see a picture of the Twin Towers and the words "Nine-eleven was just the beginning!" Please do not forget nine-eleven. It is important for America's survival that we remember the nature of the enemy and the true face of radical Islam.

I have inserted Chapter one of "*We Hold These Truths*" below. It takes place on the day of nine-eleven where four rural folks are sitting around the television watching as the Twin Towers crash to the ground. It is good to remember the past, even if it's painful. Read on and remember. Read on and honor those who died and those who struggled to save them on that dreadful day.

"I think we ought to nuke 'em, that's what I think!"

Pastor Josh McCullen interrupted him with a half-hearted rebuke. He wanted to nuke them too, but his Christian faith commanded restraint.

"Oh just calm down now Luke! We don't even know all the facts yet. Let's not rush to judgment!"

A small group of four men were huddled at a corner table in the Mudhen Grille, staring up at the television screen, watching the news reporter as he stood in front of the twin towers of the World Trade Center in New York City. Black smoke was billowing from both buildings as firemen rushed into the blaze and police officers tried to calm the people coming out.

Jack Sanders, the local garage mechanic silenced them with a tense sneer.

"Just shut up, both of you! I'm trying to hear!"

A fourth man, Henry Bolthouse, turned up the volume and they all sat grim-faced, as they listened to the sounds of mayhem and destruction.

"All we know Brian, is that at approximately 8:50AM this morning, the first of the two airliners crashed into the north tower of the World Trade Center, leaving it smoking and engulfing the top part of it in flames. We assume that all the passengers aboard were killed instantly. Then, at approximately 9 AM, the second airliner crashed into the south tower near the 80th floor. Both towers are blazing and smoking now, . . . "

The announcer hesitated, then yelled out.

"Oh my God! Did you see that! A man just jumped through a window, Brian! I saw a man jump out and land onto a car from about 50 floors up! Oh my God! Look, there's more jumping!"

The camera moved off the announcer and onto the smoking building. Tiny specks, like human bugs were clinging tenaciously to the outer wall of the building, then, one by one, they separated themselves from the burning tower and plummeted through the air to their deaths. The cameraman tried to zoom in but couldn't do it. Brian Becker then interrupted him.

"Neil, you need to get out of there. Fall back to a safer position and report from further out."

There was no answer.

"Neil, are you there?"

The camera moved back down to view Neil Champion, veteran newscaster, bent at the waist, and hugging his arms around his torso. There were tears streaming down his face and falling to the dirty pavement.

"Neil, can you talk to us?"

Neil took a deep breath, and then stood up, wiped his eyes

and began to talk again.

"Everything seems out of control here and the firefighters are concentrating on getting as many people out of the buildings as they can." He hesitated. "I'm sorry. I just never seen anyone die before. I . . . I, just don't . . . don't know what to say."

Brian Becker interrupted him, his voice sympathetic and soft.

"It's okay Neil, just tell us all what you see."

The announcer turned around and pointed to the buildings and the camera zoomed in on the top half of both towers.

"As you can see, Brian, the black smoke is getting thicker, and. . . Oh my God!"

The four men huddled at the table jumped to their feet, aghast at the sight before them.

"Oh my God! Oh my God! Brian one of the towers is coming down! Oh my God!"

"Neil, get out of there!"

A wall of dust and smoke and debris came pushing toward the camera like an unstoppable tidal wave.

"They're all dead! All those people are dead! The tower just collapsed on top of itself and a cloud of dust and smoke is coming towards us. All those people are dead!"

The men in the Mudhen Grille watched as the smoke and dust spread out across the city and eventually engulfed the news reporter. The camera jumped back and forth and the picture suddenly went black.

Pastor McCullen, blurted out in shock.

"Oh my God! They just toppled the Twin Towers! Oh God help us! All those people are dead!"

He dropped to his knees and began to pray.

Luke, the owner of the Mudhen Grille jumped up and ran over to the phone.

"My daughter works near one of those buildings! I have to make sure she's safe!"

Henry fell silent as they watched the empty screen and listened from a distance as Luke tried in vain to call his daughter in New York City.

A few seconds later a different newscaster came on the screen, filling the void.

"Ladies and gentlemen, this is Brian Becker of TV 8 news in New York City. It would appear that we have lost contact with Neil Champion who was covering the attack on the twin towers. We have no word yet as to his condition, but we can only hope and pray that he is okay and especially that most of the people inside the building were able to get out in time."

The announcer hesitated, waiting for information coming in through his earphone.

"Our sources now tell us that both World Trade Center buildings at this time of day contain approximately 10,000 people either working or visiting to do business. But of course, we have no way of knowing how many have just been killed or injured. I don't see how anyone could have survived the collapse. I just don't see it. Tears welled up in Brian Becker's eyes and the camera zoomed in on him.

"How could anyone do such a heinous thing? I don't understand. I just don't understand!"

He listened to his earpiece again and hesitated once more, then continued in a more animated voice.

"Ladies and gentlemen, we take you now to Arlington, Virginia, for a live eyewitness report, where a third airliner has crashed into the Pentagon."

Both men at the table walked around their chairs and stood transfixed in front of the television screen, their mouths dropped open gaping dumbly like big, black holes.

"I don't believe it Henry! I just don't believe it!"

Henry, a large-bodied farmer in bib overalls, about 70 years old, closed his mouth and stood resolutely in place.

"It don't surprise me none Jack. It's been a comin'."

"What do you mean?"

"You know darn well what I mean. We let ourselves get weak and it's happened again. Pearl Harbor all over again. Why don't people ever learn?"

Jack looked up at the Pentagon's broken rim, the symbol of our nation's might, burning in flames.

"My God! What's gonna happen now?"

Luke hung up the phone and walked back over.

"Can't get my daughter."

He bowed his head solemnly, the look of hope, slowly fading from his face, gradually being replaced with anger and rage. When he looked up again, his lips pursed tightly together and then he spoke with a resolute sneer.

"I'll tell you what we do - only one thing to do. We find 'em, and we nuke 'em! We're obliged to."

Henry and Jack nodded their heads in unison.

"Yep. I guess we have to. We're obliged."

I got to know Ted Nugent (the Motor City Madman, the Teditor Preditor, the Nuge) when I worked with him for almost 10 years as a Director of his organization Ted Nugent United Sportsmen of America (TNUSA). One of the nice things about Ted is that you always know where he stands. No one is indifferent about Ted. You either love him or loathe him. The anti-gunners and anti-hunters wish him dead. Ted is also fiercely loyal to his friends and his family. He was ready to come to my aid when I was being targeted by anti-Second Amendment forces here in Michigan. Ted has earned my eternal respect and friendship. Here he is in Africa with his beautiful wife Shemane on safari, where she bagged this trophy Zebra. (Photo courtesy of Ted Nugent USA.)

Chuck Perricone was the Speaker of the Michigan House of Representa-
tives back in 2000 when the CCW bill was passed. Chuck was instru-
mental in shepherding the bill through the convoluted political process
until it was finally signed into law by Governor Engler. As Michigan
State Director of Ted Nugent United Sportsmen of America, I worked
closely with Chuck on subsequent CCW law improvements. I am honored to call Chuck a staunch friend and ally. Chuck now serves as the
Executive Director of Michigan Coalition for Responsible Gun Owners (MCRGO). MCRGO is the largest and most effective state-based
pro-second Amendment organization in the United States. Go to www.
mcrgo.org to join and find out more.

The entire Nugent family has been very good to me. I owe them all a lot. Especially Ted's daughter, Sasha, who is the President of Ted Nugent United Sportsmen of America. Sasha and I worked together for many years building an organization to promote safe and responsible hunting. The Nugents are good people and family means everything to them. Like Ted always says: "Take your kids hunting, so you don't have to hunt for your kids." (Photo courtesy of Ted Nugent USA.)

The moment I became a father, something inside me clicked on. It was like a rusty door had been stuck shut my whole life and had suddenly broken free and swung open. From that moment on, I knew that my primary purpose in life was to protect my family. This is my 6-month old son, Cedar Lance Coryell. People sometimes ask me why I carry a concealed pistol. I just point to my wife and children and smile. My family depends on me to protect them from criminal, bad-guy scum. Bottom line: if you try to hurt my family, then your life is forfeit. There's nothing more to think about or say. It's automatic.

As Michigan State Director of Ted Nugent United Sportsmen of America I was proud to be the first organization to endorse Brian Calley in his campaign for State Representative of Michigan's 83rd district. Brian will make a great State Representative, and I look forward to working with him in the future. Here he is accepting a copy of my third book.

I first met Senator Alan Cropsey back in 2000 when he spoke at a Ted Nugent United Sportsmen Second Amendment rally right here in Hastings. I was very impressed with his speech on the history of CCW. When I got to know him personally, I learned that he is equally impressive as a man of character and uncompromising convictions. Alan and I share not only our Second Amendment views, but more importantly, we share a deep-seated faith in God, Family, and Country.

Craig Frank took over for me as Michigan State Director of Ted Nugent United Sportsmen of America. Craig is on fire for the Second Amendment and doing great things for our state. Originally from the Detroit area, Craig moved to the Upper Peninsula where he sells hunting land for Statewide real estate in L'Anse. My family and I visit up there several times a year and always have a great time. (Photo courtesy of Angela Frank.)

This is my hunting buddy, Staff Sergeant Bobby Napier who has just returned from 15 months in Iraq. He spent most of his time on patrol in Baghdad and training the Iraqi Police. Here he is shown in typical battle gear. It was heavy and hot with temperatures well above 100 degrees on most days. I thank God for soldiers who are willing to lay down their lives to protect the rest of us. Their sacrifice allows us to sleep safely and carry on our day-to-day lives. We owe all veterans a debt we can never repay.

Here's my good friend Dave Neeson with my 6-month old son, Cedar. Dave was my first convert to the CCW cause. Dave and I were the first to crash the County Gun Board meeting. Eventually the meetings opened up to the public, largely due to the efforts of citizen warriors like Dave. I have come to respect Dave for his willingness to serve his fellow man. Dave Neeson – the tallest man on two wheels!

Here I am with Stacie Rae, the Executive Assistant for Senator Alan Cropsey. Stacie was a beginner, but after a few hours of instruction she was right in the "stop-the-threat" zone. I had to practice to get good, but many of these women just walk up and start plinking out the bullseye. I love to see husband and wife teams attend my class. The man always walks away with a newfound respect for his wife.

Here is my wife, Sara. She's my back-up in the event things go bad. At first glance, she looks beautiful and harmless, but mess with her family and she's a mother Grizzly with cubs and a .38 revolver. More women should be like her. She is prepared. Here she is seen with her favorite carry pistol, a model 642 Smith and Wesson revolver. With +p ammo it packs a lot of punch.

Here is Sheriff Dar Leaf teaching students to shoot at a CCW class hosted by Michigan Coalition for Responsible Gun Owners. MCRGO puts classes on several times a year specifically for legislators and their staff. Once legislators take the class, they better understand the needs of CCW holders.

As Chief Pistol Instructor for Ted Nugent United Sportsmen of Michigan, I travel all across the state teaching CCW classes. All proceeds go to children's charities". This class was held in Lawrence at the home of Area Director Harold Johnson.

Michigan just passed an apprentice hunter program into law, and my 12-year old daughter is very happy. In 9 days, I will take her on her very first Whitetail Deer hunt. I think she is most excited about helping Dad feed the family. Children hunting with a parent or another responsible adult is a great introduction to firearms. It also brings families closer together and builds memories for a lifetime.

Marksmanship teaches children discipline and responsibility. In my classes, I teach the Eddie Eagle Gun Safety Program which tells children how to respond when they see an unattended firearm: "Stop! Don't touch! Leave the area! Tell an adult." I have taught this to my children with great success. Parents are the best judge of their children, and they know best when their child is ready to learn about firearms. Every child is different and should be taught on a child-by-child basis. Here is my 10-year-old son, Phillip, practicing under my supervision with a Glock airsoft pistol. He loves it.

Much of my training is scenario based. This means that I put the student in a real-life situation, then teach them different options for response. Many times, the best response is physical combat, especially when your attacker is close up. Because of this, I also teach how to disarm your attacker using the principles of physical leverage and action vs reaction.

Every time I begin a class, I tell my students this:

"I can teach you that the three main parts of a pistol are the frame, the barrel and the action. I can teach you that the parts of a pistol cartridge are the projectile, the casing, the propellant, and the primer. But none of those things will keep you alive in a gunfight or keep you out of the court system. So today I'm going to focus on teaching you how to stay alive and how to stay out of jail.

In this picture, Sheriff Dar Leaf has just bought a copy of my novel "We Hold These Truths" at a local book signing. Dar is one of those special people who remembers that the law, without common sense, is a disservice to the community. He sees himself as a servant, someone who was chosen by the people to do a dirty job that no one else wants to do. He does that job with integrity and with compassion.

The week following the Virginia Tech Massacre, Steve Deace of WHO radio, 1040 AM, in Des Moines invited me to be a guest on his afternoon drive show and I graciously accepted. Steve talked to me about my views on gun control and personal defense, and we hit it off well from the start. I am pleased to now call him my friend and fellow Christian brother. If you get a chance, go to www.whoradio. com and check out Steve's own book "*Without a Vision the People Perish*". It's an excellent read and I highly recommend it.

Roger Burdette (left) is a registered lobbyist in Des Moines for IowaCarry, Inc. He is a member of the Board of Directors and a tireless supporter for the right to keep and bear arms in Iowa. Here he is shown with State Representative Clel Baudler (right). The honorable Mr. Baudler has introduced several pro-CCW bills into the House but the climate is not yet right for passage. When the shall-issue bill is passed into law in Iowa, it will be the result of hard work by a team of dedicated individuals composed of citizen activists like IowaCarry Inc., elected officials like Representative Clel Baudler, and law enforcement supporters such as Sheriff Denniston.

When I moved to Iowa, one of my major concerns was that I would no longer be able to teach CCW in my home state. Thanks to fellow NRA Instructor, Larry Jackson, I still return to Michigan once a month to teach the good folks of Michigan how to protect themselves and their families. I consider myself fortunate to partner with an experienced instructor with the utmost integrity. I enjoy teaching with Larry very much, and I'm honored to have him. (Photo courtesy of Nancy Jackson.)

My first Iowa speaking engagement was at the IowaCarry.org annual banquet. IowaCarry is an organization devoted to bringing fair concealed carry reform to the state of Iowa. After a fantastic prime rib dinner at the Crooked Creek Shooting Preserve in Washington, Iowa, I was able to speak directly to the membership of this great organization. The highlights of my speech centered on my experiences from the political battle for "shall issue" CCW reform in Michigan and my experiences as an NRA Instructor.

To my right is Steve Hensyel who serves on the IowaCarry Board of Directors. To my left is Stu Strickland who is a moderator on the IowaCarry internet forum. Of course, the little boy in my arms is my pride and joy, my 1-year-old son, Cedar Coryell. (Photo courtesy of Naomi Fowler.)

"I was pulled over for rolling through a stop sign and when the police officer asked me for my identification, I told him I was a CCW holder and that I was carrying today, just like I'm supposed to. The officer immediately drew his pistol and pointed it at me. My two little girls were in the back seat and they were terrified!"

Law Enforcement and CCW

Some years ago, I lived in a city where the Chief of Police believed that the individual right to keep and bear arms did not exist. I remember vividly the first conversation we ever had. I had just become the Southwest Michigan Area Director for Ted Nugent United Sportsmen of America, so I took Ted's advice and went in to introduce myself to the local authorities in hopes that we could work together on some worthwhile projects to better the community. It was not to be. We were both very polite and professional, but at the end of the meeting, we were still diametrically opposed on Second Amendment issues. He told me that the Second Amendment referred to the National Guard, and not to the individual. He said that no person would ever carry in "his" town. That's odd. I thought it was my town too. One of the most striking and memorable things he said was this: "You don't have the right to own a shotgun for hunting unless the government says you can."

I was amazed. I'd never run across this attitude with any law enforcement officer before. That conversation took place many years ago, and today, a lot of people carry in "his" town. However, as it turned out, the town wasn't big enough for the both of us, so I got out of Dodge. I still respect his authority and his political views, but we'll never see eye to eye. It seems the two of us will always be at odds over the right to keep and bear arms.

Two years ago, in my own home county, we had one of the most anti-Second Amendment Sheriff's in the state. To this date, I've only had one conversation with him, and that was over the phone. I recall that I was working with Dave Stevens, a man who had created a group called Barry County Citizens for Second Amendment and Firearm Rights (BSAFR). Prior to the passage of shall issue CCW in Michigan, Dave had been working with the Sheriff, trying to get him to issue a few CCW permits to good applicants. Dave told me that the Sheriff had promised to loosen up and issue a few after his re-election. When this didn't materialize, I called him up to talk about it. The conversation started out great until I mentioned CCW. It was all downhill from there. Here is how I remember it:

"What do we have to do to get you to start issuing at least a few CCW permits here in Barry county?"

He said it was a mute point since the new law goes into effect on July 1st. I said "Hey, let's be candid here. You are working with "People Who Care about Kids" to try and block that law aren't you? He said, "Yes, what's wrong with that?" I told him that in all likelihood, they would be successful in finding an anti-Second Amendment judge on the east side of the state to block the law until December, but that waiting an entire year is unacceptable to us. He said there was nothing he could do about it. If he starts voting yes on the gun board, then he would be going against his convictions and he will never do that. I said I'd hoped we could come to some sort of agreement in order to avoid certain unpleasantries for him.

He said, "What type of unpleasantries?"

I said, "Well, recalling you for one. Starting a media campaign and giving you a lot of bad PR that could make your life very uncomfortable."

He said, "Are you threatening me?"

I said, "No, I'm promising you!"

He said, "Go ahead! Bring on the recall!"

I said, "Okay, we will!"

That was about it, other than I thanked him for returning my call. Quite frankly, I don't think I'll ever be on the man's Christmas card list. Oh well, one less thing.

There was no doubt that this man was finally admitting he was anti-CCW and that he would do whatever it took to block the new law. Later on, we did find his name on the website for "People Who Care About Kids". He was listed as a supporter of that organization's efforts to stop the new shall-issue CCW law from going into effect. They almost succeeded, but not quite.

In all my dealings with law enforcement, I've noticed that the rank and file officers seem to be supporters of the individual's right to keep and bear arms. I like that. But this doesn't appear to be true for much of the upper management segment of law enforcement. Sometimes I wonder: "Before they promote someone to a management position, do they take them into a dark room and suck out half their brain?"

I want to thank my good friend, Barry County Sheriff Dar Leaf, for helping me to keep a good attitude about law enforcement. Dar is one of those special people who remembers that the law, without common sense, is a disservice to the community. He sees himself as a servant, someone who was chosen by the people to do a dirty job that no one else wants to do. He does that job with integrity and with compassion, and he always remembers that he is accountable to the people who elected him to that position with no resentment whatsoever. Serving and protecting the public is an honor. Dar realizes that, and he never feels arrogant or abuses the power of his office. He's one of the good guys.

As the State Director of Ted Nugent United Sportsmen of America, I was pleased and honored to support Dar in his election campaign. He ran against the above-mentioned anti-CCW Sheriff and defeated him by a margin of almost two to one. Now, Sheriff Leaf teaches the legal portion of all my CCW classes, and does an outstanding job.

By and large, the vast majority of law enforcement are good people, and I get along with them just fine. In this chapter, I would like to focus on that vast majority of good guys in law enforcement, but I can't. Primarily because it's not the good guys that CCW holders need to worry about; it's that miniscule percentage of bad apples who join law enforcement either for the wrong reason, or who just don't have the temperament or good judgment for it. But it seems like there's always that "ten percent" of bad apples in every segment of our society. Law enforcement is no exception to that, though I suspect that in this case, the percentage of "bad" officers is much less than ten. Please remember, police officers are drawn from the general population, so it stands to reason that not all of them are the sharpest knives in the drawer. (Remember, there are a few bad CCW holders as well.)

Sheriff Leaf is an NRA Training Counselor, teaching the legal portion for all my CCW classes, and when he talks about civilian encounters with law enforcement, he is quick to point out: "Just because he's a cop, doesn't mean he's good at his job. Be careful."

I respect that he's able to notice and acknowledge that his own profession, just like all others, has its problems that need fixing. Power corrupts, and absolute power corrupts absolutely. High and mighty people have no business in law enforcement, but still, a few inevitably slip through the cracks.

A few months ago I was teaching a CCW class and one of my renewal students told this story.

"I was pulled over for rolling through a stop sign and when the police officer asked me for my identification, I told him I was a CCW holder and that I was carrying today, just like I'm supposed to. The officer immediately drew his pistol and pointed it at me. My two little girls were in the back seat and they were terrified! He put me facedown on the hood of my car and disarmed me."

I was shocked by this man's story, and I spent the next 15 minutes of class trying to calm down the other students, assuring them that this was unusual and that most police officers would treat them with dignity and respect. But it's true, a few bad apples will spoil it for the whole bunch.

Last month I taught a CCW class to Michigan state legislators and their staff. It is part of an initiative by Michigan Coalition for Responsible Gun Owners (MCRGO) to educate the people who make the laws and to give them a greater understanding of what it's like to be a CCW holder. I especially like teaching law enforcement and legislators, because inevitably, they walk away realizing they have nothing to fear from CCW holders. We're just honest, law-abiding citizens who want to protect our families. During the break, I was talking to a State Representative who told me he was taking the class, but would not be applying for his concealed pistol license. I was surprised and asked him why. He said, "A friend of mine was hauled out of his car and treated roughly for being a CCW holder and I don't want that to happen to me."

I was amazed at his statement. Here was a legislator who was afraid of being abused by law enforcement for following a law he had helped to make. That didn't make sense to me.

But it does show that the fear of police officers is engrained in us all. To some extent, it's a very healthy and necessary thing. Criminals should be afraid of law enforcement. That's what we, as a society, want to happen. But the rest of us, the vast majority of the population who are honest, law-abiding citizens, we should have no reason to fear the police so long as we follow the law. After all, we're on the same team.

But still . . . a man walks up to your car at night with a gun. He has the power to handcuff you, search you, arrest you, and throw you in jail. That sounds extreme, and it is, but I'm discovering that many people, even legislators, view law enforcement in that light.

Law enforcement has a tough job. There's no denying that. But a few dull knives in their ranks make it a lot tougher on all of us. Let's face it, some of these laws are idiotic, senseless, while others are just downright wrong. Just because it's the law, doesn't mean it's right. I always obey the law, but when I find one I don't agree with, I work hard to get it changed or abolished. That was the case with CCW; the old "may issue" law was wrong, so ordinary citizens like you and I fought long and hard to get it changed. Remember slavery and women's suffrage? They were undeniably wrong and immoral, and no reasonable person would defend them in today's society. The world isn't flat anymore.

In my experience, the vast majority of law enforcement has used common sense in applying the law. But as in everything, it's the "gomers", the "no-loads", and the "boneheads" that people remember. I can be pulled over ten times and be treated with dignity and respect for nine out of ten of those traffic stops, but it's the one time I was abused that will stick in my mind forever. That may not be right, but it is human nature.

I think for the most part that both legislators and law enforcement have the best of intentions, but that doesn't mean that they're always "good at their jobs". I disagree with the helmet law, the seatbelt law, and most recently the cell phone law. In fact, I take issue with any law that empowers the government to protect people from their own stupidity. The stupid ones aren't going to buckle up no matter how many laws you pass, and the rest of us, the smart ones, we already buckle up.

And there is always that small segment in law enforcement who become overzealous in trying to protect us from ourselves. I get very concerned when I see five state police cruisers lined up on the side of the road, one trooper with binoculars, another with a radio, looking for people who are talking on their cell phones. They call these banes to freedom "enforcement zones" and they even put up a big sign to that effect. This reminds me of those old World War II movies where the Nazi storm troopers would stop people and demand to see their papers.

Shouldn't they be using those binoculars to find drug dealers, muggers, and rapists? I think we would all feel safer if they did.

In closing, let me reiterate my support for law enforcement. I would draw my pistol and defend any police officer in need. I want to thank the vast majority of the police who protect us from crime and spend day in and day out doing a dirty, thankless job. I know it's tough out there on the streets.

I wish that all police officers could take my CCW class. It would help to reassure them that the vast majority of CCW holders are good people who just want to protect their families. And it would help reassure the CCW holders that the police are just doing their job and want to return safely at night to their wife and kids.

People fear what they don't know and don't understand. My wish is that law enforcement and the CCW holder can come together and understand each other's perspectives and points of view. To that small segment of law enforcement who feels threatened by CCW holders, please remember this. All of us jumped through a lot of hoops, spent money, filled out forms, took training classes, and waited, just to reacquire our right to keep and bear arms. Don't be afraid of us. We are the law-abiding citizens. We're on your side. We're the ones who would draw our own guns to protect you from the bad guys. I'm not asking you to let down your guard, just that you treat us with respect.

And to the small percentage of CCW holders who have developed a bad attitude about law enforcement, I ask you to reevaluate your stance. Don't shoot the messengers, no pun intended. If you don't like a law, then fight politically to change it. Find out who the bad legislators are and vote them out of office. If you're not politically active, then you have no right to complain. The police are the good guys; they're sheep dogs just like you and I. So treat them with respect.

Thanks again to Sheriff Leaf and all the good guys in law enforcement. You put your life on the line for the rest of us, and we thank you. May God keep you safe. Y'all can sit by my fire anytime.

The mob became nasty and broke out windows in Dr. Sweet's home and pelted his roof with rocks. The size of the mob was estimated to be in the hundreds. Someone from inside Dr. Sweet's home fired shots from a gun, and a white man named Leon Breiner was killed.

The OK Corral

"A long time ago, in a galaxy far, far away, people had the right to keep and bear arms ...."

I think that's how a lot of us felt here in Michigan, prior to year 2000 and the passage of Public Act 381, the statute which finally allowed us to carry a concealed pistol here in Michigan for lawful purposes. Prior to that, Concealed Pistol Licenses to ordinary citizens were few and far between. The most notable exceptions were a few rural counties in Northern Michigan and over in Macomb County, which adopted "shall issue" type standards back in the 1990s.

But for the vast majority of us, it was quite simply, "have a nice day, drive safely, but leave your pistola at home." It was a felony, and even those few who dared to carry for moral purposes, e.g., self-defense, family defense, etc., were risking a felony conviction, loss of firearm ownership, and loss of voting rights. Quite frankly, it wasn't worth it. And while many of us were infuriated and righteously indignant over the loss of our Second Amendment rights, I never met anyone within the cause who violated the ill-conceived legislation, even for the purpose of self-defense - myself included. This is a credit to the honesty and integrity of all the men and women who fought for the cause. If ever a law cried out to be violated, it was

Michigan's old CCW law. It was, without a doubt, ill-conceived, immoral and unconstitutional.

But I am a devout Christian, and the Bible teaches me to respect the law and those charged with enforcing it. So I did, begrudgingly. I was taught that if a law is wrong, a person should change it – not break it. So, together, the Second Amendment supporters throughout our great state, banded together and fought to right the wrong, to regain our civil liberty and our God-given inalienable right to keep and bear arms.

Thank God we didn't know how long it was going to take! Thank God we didn't know how much personal sacrifice and above-and-beyond the call effort it was going to demand from our families and ourselves. But, when all was said and done, the honest, law-abiding citizens of Michigan were once again allowed to carry concealed pistols for defense of themselves and the state. Happy ending!

But, before we jump that far ahead, let's first examine the course of human events and the circumstances that led up to how we got into such a fine kettle of fish in the first place.

> *"The price of freedom is eternal vigilance."*
> *– Thomas Jefferson –*

No saying ever rang more true. If there's one thing I've learned over the past 10 years, "it's easier to defend a right than it is to regain one that's been lost". Those military veterans out there will understand this concept all too well. In fact, some of you may have learned it the hard way, through the shedding of blood, in service to our beloved country. It takes more lives to recapture a hill than to successfully defend it.

Never give your adversary the high ground. Hold on to it for dear life, and never give your adversary time to dig in and set up defenses.

A long time ago, in 1927, we the people of Michigan, unwittingly and short-sightedly, violated both these two timeless cardinal rules of warfare.

For instructional purposes, and to help illustrate my point, let's just take a few minutes to summarize the roots of gun control laws.

For all practical purposes, gun control wasn't a major factor in the United States until after the Civil War. During that time, generally known to historians as the Reconstruction Period, the first dangerous gun control laws began cropping up. And, ironically, these first gun control laws had their roots in the Deep South, where the Second Amendment and the use of firearms is championed and defended in today's world. Who would have ever thought that gun control would originate in the South, a venerable fortress of patriotism and constitutionality. But it did. And life nationwide may never be the same again.

Prior to the Civil War Reconstruction Period, gun control consisted primarily of checking your pistol at the door upon entering the saloon. Some major cities even had city ordinances, which prohibited the carrying of firearms within the city limits. This, however, was the exception, and not the rule. In fact, even prior to the Civil war, during the Antebellum period of history, gun laws were passed sporadically throughout the South, mostly in an effort to keep guns out of the hands of slaves and freed slaves.

But the new gun laws in the South after the Civil War were of a different spirit, not rooted in the desire for safety, but rather in hatred, bigotry, and racism. These new laws were called "Jim Crow" laws, and they were designed to deprive newly freed slaves of their civil rights. The general attitude was: "The federal government may be able to emancipate them, but that doesn't mean we have to treat them as equals!"

As in many cases, these racist attitudes were rooted in fear, resentment, and bitterness. They had lost the war, and they didn't much like it! Some had mistreated their slaves, and feared retaliation from their former "property". It was also much easier for night riders and the KKK to oppress former slaves when they were unable to shoot back. So, to deal with the problem, and to get around federal laws and the U.S. Constitution, Southern state and local governments passed laws, which prohibited certain classes of people from possessing firearms. They also passed laws, which, refused blacks the right to vote, and from using the same facilities as Whites. But they were forced to be underhanded about it. They just couldn't pass a law that said, "Black people can't vote." That was way too obvious and wouldn't have been tolerated by the Federal government. They had to phrase it differently. For example, "Anyone not able to pass a written exam, is incapable of voting intelligently and responsibly, and therefore cannot vote."

Clayton Cramer, noted historian and author of such books as "Firing Back" and "Concealed Weapon Laws of the Early Republic: Dueling, Southern Violence, and Moral Reform" summed it up best in the following quote from his paper in the Kansas Journal of Law and Public Policy. The paper was titled "The Racist Roots of Gun Control"

The entire paper can be found at the following web address: http://www.lizmichael.com/racistro.htm

"The end of slavery in 1865 did not eliminate the problems of racist gun control laws; the various Black Codes adopted after the Civil War required blacks to obtain a license before carrying or possessing firearms or Bowie knives; these are sufficiently well-known that any reasonably complete history of the Reconstruction period mentions them. These restrictive gun laws played a part in the efforts of the Republicans to get the Fourteenth Amendment ratified, because it was difficult for night riders to generate the correct level of terror in a victim who was returning fire. It does appear, however, that the requirement to treat blacks and whites equally before the law led to the adoption of restrictive firearms laws in the South that were equal in the letter of the law, but unequally enforced. It is clear that the vagrancy statutes adopted at roughly the same time, in 1866, were intended to be used against blacks, even though the language was race-neutral. The former states of the Confederacy, many of which had recognized the right to carry arms openly before the Civil War, developed a very sudden willingness to qualify that right. One especially absurd example, and one that includes strong evidence of the racist intentions behind gun control laws, is Texas."

So, you see, much of gun control in the United States is deeply rooted in racism. But don't take my word for it. Go to www.barnesandnoble.com to order Clayton Cramer's books on the subject. He has studied the matter extensively and has included meticulous documentation and footnoting to back up his thesis.

Over the years and decades, this racist attitude and subsequent anti-black laws, began to creep their way north. Eventually, it reached the northern state of Michigan on September 9th, 1925.

On that day, a mob of white people, who called themselves the "Waterworks Improvement Association", marched on the home of a black American named Dr. Ossian Sweet, who had just moved into a white affluent neighborhood in the city of Detroit. (At the time, the KKK claimed to have 100,000 members in the city of Detroit.) The mob became nasty and broke out windows in Dr. Sweet's home and pelted his roof with rocks. The size of the mob was estimated to be in the hundreds. Someone from inside Dr. Sweet's home fired shots from a gun, and a white man named Leon Breiner was killed. (Later on, Dr. Sweet's brother, Henry, admitted to firing the shots.) All eleven black people inside Dr. Sweet's home were arrested. Prosecutor Robert M. Toms charged them all with murder.

But, even then, things were not to go the way of the Klan. To the casual onlooker, it appeared as if Dr. Sweet would soon be bumping butts with Big Bubba in the shower, praying that he never dropped the soap. And he probably would have ended up in prison, had it not been for a famous lawyer named Clarence Darrow who came to his rescue.(Mr. Darrow became famous for his part in the Scopes Monkey trial, which allowed evolution to be taught in school in July of 1925.)

"I have to die a man or live a coward."
− Dr. Ossian Sweet, 1925 −

In a dramatic and well publicized trial, Dr. Sweet and the other 10 black defendants were acquitted of all wrongdoing. The County Prosecutor then went after Dr. Sweet's brother, Henry, but was unsuccessful there as well. The presiding Judge, a young man named Frank Murphy, made it clear to the jury that the right to defend one's home applied to blacks as well as to whites.

The outcome of the second trial infuriated the KKK and other racist whites even more. Once again, they brought their considerable political strength to bear. This time not against just Mr. Sweet, but against every Black American in the state of Michigan. As a result, Michigan Public Act 372 was passed and went into effect on September 5th, 1927. Similar to the Jim Crow laws of the South, it merely said "If the County Gun Board deems the applicant a suitable candidate, then they may issue them a permit to carry a concealed pistol". This "may issue" law, on the surface, appeared to have nothing of a racial nature, but appearances can sometimes be deceiving. Giving the County Gun Board (composed of the County Prosecutor, County Sheriff, and the State Police) sole and unquestionable power to either grant or deny concealed pistol licenses, opened the entire system up to corruption and later elitism. It created two classes of citizen: the "haves" and the "have nots".

Initially, this didn't cause widespread problems. Almost anyone could still apply for and receive a concealed pistol license, unless of course, you were black. But, gradually, the spirit of bigotry, racism, and elitism took root and began to fester and grow. Because the law was so subjective and vague, setting no uniform standards or criteria for issuance, it wasn't long before all 83 of the county gun boards were doing things differently. The Pandora's box of bigotry and hatred had been opened, and nothing short of legislative overhaul would again close it. Some gun boards began denying CPLs to Catholics, some to Protestants, some to Hispanics, others to Italian or Irish Immigrants. The list was unending, limited only by man's own ability to discriminate against his fellow citizen.

Later on, the list of "have nots" was to grow even larger, until finally, circa 1970, only law enforcement, or prior law enforcement were ensured their right to keep and bear arms, in most counties. All others, with the exception of those who were friends of the Sheriff or Prosecutor, were routinely denied Concealed Pistol Licenses altogether. After a period of years, people ceased to even apply, and in some cases began to believe the elitist stance that "you may

have the right to own a gun, but only for home defense or hunting."
This proved to be a very slippery slope. Eventually, certain people
in positions of power came to believe and espouse that the Second
Amendment applied only to the National Guard, a view which is
in direct contradiction with all the correspondence of the founding
fathers as well as the Federalist Papers.

But then in 1979 a young champion appeared in the form of a
tall, skinny State Representative named Alan Cropsey. Mr. Cropsey
sponsored the first "shall issue" CCW bill in the state of Michigan.
He fought hard to pass the bill, but it was not to be. Mr. Cropsey was
term-limited out of office before his bill was passed. (Alan Cropsey,
now a State Senator, is generally considered to be the grandfather of
CCW reform in Michigan.)

But the fight was not over. A fire had been lit, and the flames of
freedom were fanned all across the state. Ordinary people fought
long and hard to regain their right to keep and bear arms, and finally,
on January 2nd, 2001, Governor John Engler signed Public Act 381
into law. It went into effect on July 1st of 2001, after an unsuccessful
6-month court battle by the anti-gun group "People who care about
Kids".

In July, the first "shall issue" CCW permit was issued in Barry
County. The following month, approximately 30 more were issued.
Today, there are over 6,000 CCW holders in Barry county, a rural
farming county with a population of only 40,000 adults over the age
of 21. (According to the 2000 census.) I am proud that 15 percent
of our adult citizens are sheep dogs, and that the number is growing
every month. I'm proud to be a part of that, and I'm proud to be the
one who trains them to be safe shepherds of the flock.

I've always found it humorous, though slightly sad, that the
anti-Second Amendment crowd warned us for years that if the bill

passed into law, there would be "Blood in the Streets". We would all die. All of us nonviolent, law-abiding citizens would suddenly, and inexplicably turn into cold-blooded killers. And there were always the inevitable references to road rage, shoot-outs just like in the Old West, and Dodge City.

So I got to wondering about the Old West, and I did some checking on it. I enjoy history, and I figured the left was wrong about everything else, so maybe they were wrong about the Old West as well. Here is what I found out.

It seems the Old West was more like "*Little House on the Prairie*" than the shootout at the OK Corral. Here are the statistics for some of the roughest, toughest, and most violent cattle towns in the Old West. They were taken from Robert Dykstra's book "*The Cattle Towns*". I think you'll be surprised.

	Dodge	Abilene	Ellsworth	Caldwell	Wichita	Total Homicides
1870	0	2	0	0	0	2
1871	0	3	0	0	1	4
1872	0	2	1	0	1	4
1873	0	0	5	0	1	6
1874	0	0	0	0	1	1
1875	0	0	0	0	0	0
1876	0	0	0	0	0	0
1877	0	0	0	0	0	0
1878	5	0	0	0	0	5
1879	2	0	0	2	0	4
1880	1	0	0	2	0	3
1881	1	0	0	2	0	3
1882	1	0	0	3	0	4
1883	0	0	0	1	0	1
1884	3	0	0	2	0	5
1885	2	0	0	1	0	3
Total	15	7	6	13	4	45

Other historians and authors agree that the unbridled reports of violence of the Old West is largely a myth. Of course, there were isolated examples of violence, but the true story of the American West was one of cooperation, not gunfights in the open streets, lynchings and murder. That's just Hollywood. Let's face it, Clint Eastwood does better at the box office than Grizzly Adams. Stephen King has better book sales than Hugo Martini. And you may ask, "Who's Hugo Martini? That's my point. No one knows, because no one reads his work. (Sorry Hugo.) Why do people read Stephen King? Because his characters and plot lines are interesting. They're about lunatics, murderers, and supernatural maniacs and sociopaths. Perish the thought, but 100 years from now people will be reading

Stephen King's book "*The Shining*" and thinking, Wow, people were crazy back then. Sure am glad I didn't live in that time period. Are there really people out there like King's characters? Sadly enough, yes, but they are few and far between.

I'm sorry anti-gunners, but the Old West was very boring and "safe" by the standards of today's cities. Dodge City, reputed to be the roughest, toughest, most dangerous city in the Old West, had a total of 15 homicides during its hay day between 1870 and 1885. That's an average of one per year. So where would you rather live, present day Detroit or the Old West in Dodge City? I'll take Dodge every time. Detroit makes me nervous, and Chicago and D.C. are downright terrifying.

So, you can see that the blood in the streets of the Old West was a myth, propagated by Hollywood and others in the media in order to boost book and box office sales. Likewise, the blood in the streets that the anti-gunners are currently prophesying in Wisconsin is nothing short of a lie. It's a tool they use to scare ignorant people into supporting their political agenda.

So what's the lesson here? Stop being lazy! Get off your butt and read and research. Find out the truth instead of passively accepting the bloated breast of the left, suckling on the tainted milk of their infected, intellectually barren mammary glands. (Oh my! That paints a not so pretty picture. Leaves a nasty taste in my mouth too.)

Grow up people! Educate yourselves and hold your leaders and their willing accomplices in the media accountable. After all, we are "We the people". Let's start acting that way.

Jesus himself was the most politically incorrect, offensive, person on the planet. In fact, he spoke his mind and was crucified for it by the people who took offense.

The PC Gestapo

Political correctness is the bastion of liberalism, and the bane of American free thought and speech. So much of modern day idiocy can be laid to rest simply by asking this one question: "What would your grandfather have said about it?"

I can see it now.

"I'm sorry Grandpa, but you can't use the word 'mankind'."

Grandpa would cock his head to one side and ask, "Why not?"

"Because it's sexist and an insult to women."

Grandpa would narrow his eyes and look at you with that omniscient, patriarchal stare.

"I'll use what words I want to use, boy! And don't be giving me any crap about it, or I'll tan your hide! I'll be darned if I'm gonna let anybody tell me what I can say and what I can't say. This is America!"

I love my grandpa, God rest his soul. He had a way of cutting through all the crap and just telling it like it was. Grandpa grew up in a time when people could speak their mind, and they were allowed to choose their own words without political and social condemnation. I remember my grandpa well. He was a chain smoker and an alcoholic, and he had some strong opinions, which he voiced on occasion. Finally, after two strokes, his entire vocabulary was re-duced to one four-letter word: "Damn!" It didn't matter what I said to him. I would ask a stupid, typical teenage question, and I could see the intelligence in his eyes turn to frustration as he tried to form the sentence on his lips. In the end, all that came out was "Damn". Sometimes it came out like a shotgun in one powerful blast, while at others, it came out like a machine gun: "Damn! Damn! Damn! Damn! Damn! Damn! Damn! Damn!"

It was a hard thing to watch him in his reduced capacity. I could see the independence and intelligence in his old eyes, but he just couldn't get out the words. It used to drive my grandmother crazy to hear him cuss on full auto. But my grandpa was old school, and no one told him what to say or how to say it. I like that about old people.

And I must be getting old too, because I don't cotton much to people telling me what words I can use, and what words I can't. Doesn't that sound a bit like censorship? My children once came to me and tried to correct me on inappropriate words I was using. I responded to them by saying, "Shut up. I'm your father and I'll say what I want to say." They were appalled, and immediately launched into a diatribe about what their teacher had taught them at school. I gave them a loving diatribe of my own, and they were quick to get the message. "Don't censor Daddy."

Up until recently, I worked for a major corporation. They were a government defense contractor and had to follow a multitude of gov-ernment regulations, one of them being politically correct speech. They asked me to edit a corporate training program on harassment, which I did. They defined harassment as any word or action that of-fends another person. It upset me so much that I almost didn't make it through the training program emotionally intact.

It is impossible to keep from offending everyone. I offend people everyday. That probably didn't surprise you. However, I don't do it just to hurt people. In fact, as a Christian, I should try to not offend people. However, it's important to note that Jesus himself was the most politically incorrect, offensive, person on the planet. In fact, he spoke his mind and was crucified for it by the people who took offense. There's a country and western song by Aaron Tippin that says, "You've got to stand for something, or you'll fall for anything." Jesus stood for love, and he fell at the hands of the Pharisees who had him crucified for saying things they didn't like. I like Jesus. He was the original rebel. Jesus made James Dean look like a sissy. No one censored Jesus. And he's my hero. No one improved the world more than Jesus.

And yet, the Political Correctness Gestapo are alive and well on planet Earth and doing all the damage they can. After a short hiatus following September 11th, they started poking their furry, little heads up out of their tiny burrows and testing the wind to see if it was safe to come on out and play. I think they were infuriated by thousands of Americans who ran out and bought guns to protect themselves over the fear of terrorist attack. I recently read the following news reports which really ruffled my feathers.

"Broken Arrow, Oklahoma School officials remove
"God Bless America" signs from schools in fear
that someone might be offended."

"Channel 12 News in Long Island, New York,
orders flags removed from the newsroom and red,
white, and blue ribbons removed from the lapels of
reporters. "

"Berkeley, California bans U.S. Flags from being displayed on city fire trucks because they didn't want to offend anyone in the community."

Now I've always considered myself a reasonable man, tolerant of other people's religious and political views. After all, that's how I was raised, but this one is really stretching the limits of my patience. So after reading these headlines, I gathered my wits and thought about it for a while before taking up my pen. However, after careful deliberation, I realized that I am not willing to drink from this tainted cup of tolerance or to sacrifice everything I hold dear on the sacrilegious altar of political correctness!

Those people in Broken Arrow, what can I say about them? Their arrows may not be broken, but they're certainly twisted. And one thing I've learned in my lifetime of bow hunting, a twisted arrow will never fly straight; will always miss the mark; and will never be true.

And the people from Channel 12 News in New York City should be ashamed of their linguine-spined lack of courage. They watched and filmed as the twin towers crumbled, burned, and then rose again in a cloud of dust, blood and ashes. And what lesson did they learn from this? Did it rekindle their fire of patriotism? No! Did it serve as a personal, spiritual epiphany and bring them closer to God the Creator? No!

Throughout my 48 years, I've learned that all of life can be boiled down into two simple questions: "Who is my master – and – How can I best serve Him?"

When superimposed onto the people of Broken Arrow, Berkley, and News 12, it all makes perfect sense. Quite simply put, they serve a different master than most patriotic Americans, the ones who do most of the living, working, breathing, suffering and dying in this great country of ours.

And in Berkley, California, they serve a different master altogether: the God of Tolerance. They sit enthroned high above the rest of us common folk in their ivory towers of "higher education", spewing out their liberal, brain-dead doctrine of political correctness, all the while demonizing and pronouncing guilt upon anyone who does not conform and espouse their views. (In reality, they worship the god of tolerance, but are the most intolerant people of all.) They shackle innocent people with labels that ruin careers and shatter families. To those who believe homosexuality is a sin, they are labeled as "homophobes". To those who believe that women and men were created equal but different by God, they are labeled as "repressive sexists". To those who like to hunt and shoot, they are labeled as "gun-toting" rednecks. And to those who believe that Jesus Christ is the Son of God, they are labeled as the most intolerant and hateful of all.

Well, I for one am sick and tired of these demeaning and disgusting labels, and I think it's time we all stood up, shoulder to shoulder and said NO MORE! I can label myself, thank you, because no one knows me better than yours truly! I have strong beliefs. I'm a compassionate man, a man of conviction and promise. I say what I mean and mean what I say! Believing that homosexuality is wrong and unnatural, doesn't make me a homophobe, because my beliefs are not based on any imagined fear, but on the Word of God. But at the same time, neither does it make me better than anyone else. We're all imperfect and in need of divine help. Believing that men and women were created equal but different, doesn't make me a sexist; it makes me a realist. I'm not going to pretend that women and men are the same just to keep the noisiest 5 percent of the population from bestowing an ugly label on the remaining 95. And I don't believe that humanity has spent the last 10,000 years struggling to the top of the food chain just to become vegetarians. And most important of all, living for Jesus Christ doesn't make me intolerant, it makes me strong, and loving and compassionate.

So I do hereby solemnly and officially reject all politically correct labels. The PC Police can kiss my ... as you were, Skip. Calm down now.

I guess what I'm trying to say is that tolerance has its place, but should never be elevated above America's love for God, Family and Country. Even in the complex game of geopolitical correctness, patriotism trumps tolerance. And of course, God trumps all; because He is over all. He was not contained in the twin towers, and He did not crumble and die with that violent, despicable act of murder on September 11th. In closing, God still reigns from Heaven, despite any label the PC police may bestow upon Him.

Here are my labels. I'm a father! I'm a patriot! I'm a Christian! And I will not tolerate any label to the contrary! Get used to it PC police! Perhaps you should become more tolerant of us!

God bless America! Praise the Lord, and pass the ammunition!

Get your butt off the fence. Do the right thing. It's time to rebel!

Blood in the Streets

You have two seconds to look a stranger in the face and answer this question: Does he just want my money? or, Does he also want to kill me? Not even Freud could make that determination correctly.

The Problem of Stress

There is an old saying, "The bear would have caught me, but he slipped in my shit."

Funny things happen when we add stress to our lives, and there are certainly different kinds of stress. There is the chronic stress of working at a job you hate with a deplorable boss, and there is the stress you feel when a man jumps out from behind a car and sticks a gun in your face. It's the latter stress that we're concerned with in the personal protection arena, so let's focus on that now.

I have been a soccer official for 15 years now, and I can still remember my first game. I was scared to death. There I was, out there in the middle of the field, all by myself, surrounded by players and coaches and people who hated me. Nothing I did or said seemed to make those people happy, and everytime I blew my whistle, at least half of them were dissatisfied. But despite my fear, the lump in my throat (which turned out to be my heart) and the adrenaline coursing through my veins, I made it through that first game.

In retrospect, that's all I had to do. You're not supposed to be good at something you've never done before. All you have to do is make it through that first time, and then build on your newfound experience. During that first game, all I had to do was survive. And

2,000 games later, I'm still going strong.

It's the same way with personal protection. There is no such thing as the perfect gunfight. You will make mistakes; that's what stress does to you. All you have to do is live. With that in mind, let's take a look at what happens during a life or death situation.

The first thing that happens is your heart rate skyrockets. This is due to a huge amount of adrenaline that your body dumps into your bloodstream in anticipation of a fight. My "at rest" heart rate is about 60 beats per minute. That's fairly slow. But things quickly change when stress is added. When the adrenaline surge happens, I can feel it immediately, and it's almost impossible to control it once it's started.

When your pulse gets up to about 90, that's when your brain is functioning at its best. You are on high alert status, and there is extra oxygen being pumped to your brain and the rest of your body. But once the heart rate gets above 100, nasty things start to happen.

As soon as your brain realizes that you are in danger, it constricts the blood vessels leading to your extremities. This is done, so that if you are cut, for example on your arm, then it will take longer for you to bleed to death, and you can defend yourself for a longer period of time. Because of the lack of blood in your hands, your wrists may tingle and your fingers may feel a certain amount of numbness. Suddenly, very simple things, like ejecting a magazine, or even pulling back a slide, can become very difficult to do.

Your brain is also affected; it reverts to a primitive state of mind, where complex thinking and reasoning is next to impossible. At this point, most people can think but one thing: "Oh my god! That's a gun! I'm going to die!"

Yet, despite all these physiological realities coming into play, it is still possible for you to survive a gun fight. If you can control them, harness them, then all these things will work for you. However, if you allow the adrenaline, increased pulse, and oxygen supply to run rampant with no thought to self control, then you will be reduced to a throbbing mass of blood, spit, and urine. You are useless to yourself and a danger to your family.

So what is the answer? How do I survive? Well, a lot of it is just, plain, dumb luck. I know a lot of instructors wouldn't say that. They like to feel that their teaching can save lives, and they want their students to feel safe and secure and capable of warding off attack. I want those things too, but I would be derelict in my duties as a personal protection instructor if I didn't tell the whole truth.

The truth is, every scenario is different. Some are survivable. Others are not. I know you didn't want to hear that, but I have to tell you that sometimes it is very difficult to survive an attack, even when you do everything right. This is especially true at close range. Anyone can get off a lucky shot from 5 feet away. You don't even have to aim. And since there is no such thing as a long-distance mugging or a long-distance rape, then where does that leave us? Are we helpless victims, sheep waiting to be sheared?

Of course not. I just want you to be aware of what really happens in a gunfight so that you're not taken by surprise when it occurs. In my advanced CCW class, I show my students quite a few video tapes of real fire fights. I want them to know what it looks like and what it sounds like. I want them to see how the victim reacted. Did they freeze? Did they comply? Did they fight back?

In one of the videos, a man enters a convenience store and shoves a gun in the clerk's ribs and demands money. The clerk complies with every demand, but before the robber leaves, he shoots the man three times in the chest. During the last 30 seconds of the video, we listen as the clerk moans on the floor. Finally, his body begins to shut down and he dies.

That is sick and disgusting. Why do I subject my students to this? For two reasons: First, it lets everyone in the class know that this isn't just fun and games. This is serious and they need to pay strict attention or they too could be moaning on the floor, listening to their own throat relax into a death rattle. Second, it tells us that no matter what response you take, you can still die. When you comply to the demands of a robber with a gun, you are trusting that he will not hurt you.

This latter response has never made sense to me, because the robber has already demonstrated apathy for your life by pointing a deadly weapon at you. By complying with his demands, you are exhibiting an unfounded trust that he will do what's in your best interest. I realize that sometimes all the bad guy wants is your money, but how do you know? You have two seconds to look a stranger in the face and answer this question: Does he just want my money? or, Does he also want to kill me? Not even Freud could make that determination correctly.

In my opinion, total compliance, in most cases, is just another form of denial. I admire the writings of Lt. Colonel Dave Grossman, and I recommend that all of you read as much of him as you can. In his essay *"On Sheep, Sheepdogs, and Wolves"* he makes the following statement:

> *"We know that the sheep live in denial, which is what makes them sheep. They do not want to believe that there is evil in the world. They can accept the fact that fires can happen, which is why they want fire extinguishers, fire sprinklers, fire alarms and fire exits throughout their kids' schools.*

But many of them are outraged at the idea of putting an armed police officer in their kid's school. Our children are thousands of times more likely to be killed or seriously injured by school violence than fire, but the sheep's only response to the possibility of violence is denial. The idea of someone coming to kill or harm their child is just too hard, and so they chose the path of denial."

To the store clerk who chose to say "Baa" and live his life like a sheep, he paid the supreme price – his own life. He was shot three times in the chest at close range and died in a pool of his own blood. It is so sad to die unprepared. In five minutes I could have shown him how to save his life, at least give him a fighting chance. But most people are sheep and they cannot handle the "idea" that the world is dangerous. The realization that the world is violent, coupled with the knowledge that they are not prepared to protect themselves is overwhelming to them. They shut down, deny, and withdraw from reality.

But there is a second video that shows a store clerk sitting behind a different counter. A man walks in with a gun, and the clerk immediately drops down behind the counter, draws his gun and is waiting for the bad guy who jumps over the counter to get at him. The clerk shoots and so does the robber. Both are hit from point-blank range, but when the smoke clears the room, the clerk is left standing and the bad guy has fled.

I am convinced that one of the best ways to overcome stress is to be prepared. That clerk knew what he was going to do before the robber came through that ill-fated door. He reacted without thinking, because he'd been visualizing that scenario. Remember, we all live or die based on the decisions we make, and that clerk make the right decision and lived. The first clerk was a sheep and he died. The second clerk lived, because he was a well prepared sheep dog.

Training is paramount in a life or death struggle. You have to know what a gun fight is like before you can prepare for it, and that's why I also use airsoft pistols to simulate firefights. This tells me what works and what doesn't. I remember when I first used airsoft simulations, that I was very surprised at how easy it is to be shot and killed from close range. I dueled repeatedly with a friend of mine who had just returned from a year of fighting in Iraq. In these simulations, he killed me almost everytime, usually with a shot between the eyes. I'm a pretty good shot, so this confused me until I realized that it was the stress factor that gave him the edge. He'd been living in a life or death situation for a year and therefore had become desensitized to the stress. While an airsoft simulation is stressful for most civilians, for him it was a walk in the park.

So I've taken to desensitizing all my students to the effects of stress. This will help keep them alive in a real firefight. In my advanced class, they shoot a combat course that is full of surprises, because I want them to experience and overcome the startle response. That startle response will get you killed every time. You can't be surprised. You have to walk around every day knowing that you will be attacked and exactly what you will do to defend yourself.

I teach this even in my basic CCW class. I have them begin, one at a time on top of a hill, and they run down to their firearm, load it, get behind cover, then issue a challenge command before shooting. They do this in front of the rest of the class, while I follow behind them, yelling at their backs like a drill instructor. I add stress, and they shake, and drool, and fumble. Even the calmest of my basic students are reduced to a puddle of puke. They make the simplest mistakes: they drop the magazine, they forget to take the safety off, they forget to yell the challenge command, they forget how to clear a jam, and they put their offhand thumb behind the slide, only to have it cut and bleed. Am I being too hard on them? Maybe. (Surprisingly, this is by far the most popular portion of the class, with many of them asking to go again.) But I take the responsibility of training them seriously, so my training has to be equally serious. I don't want them walking out of there with a false sense of security. I want them to know how vulnerable they are, and I want them to realize that the basic class is just that – basic. All it does is give them a rudimentary understanding of how and when to shoot. Where they go from there is up to them. With the basic class and a healthy dose of luck, my students will survive.

But if you really want to raise your chances of survival, then you have to go to the next level. You have to train as much as you can. Put yourself in stressful situations. Desensitize yourself to the startle response. Shoot combat courses, take advanced classes, compete formally. Put yourself under stress and learn to control your heart rate and your breathing. All these are paramount to survival, and put you head and shoulders above the bad guys.

Remember, bad guys don't train, but the good guys do. Always be ready. Always be on guard. Raise your level of capability and you'll raise your chances of survival.

Women have greater need of a firearm, because they are at greater risk. Most honest, law-abiding men will never be raped, but women have no such reassurance.

Women and Guns

I find it amazing that many of the women in my basic classes can consistently outshoot the men. My classes are approximately 25 percent women and 75 percent men. Most of the women are new to firearms, whereas, most of the men have been shooting their entire lives.

So, how is it that these novices, after only a few hours of training, can sometimes outshoot the experienced men? I don't know, but, as a man, I find it frustrating. I had to practice to get good, but many of these women just walk up and start plinking out the bullseye. Life can be so cruel.

Nonetheless, while the man part of me is frustrated, the teacher part of me is pleased and likes to see it happen. I so much wish that more women would become CCW holders, because they need the added protection of a gun. Some people call women the weaker sex. That's absurd. I've watched three women birth a total of 5 kids, and I can tell you that any woman who can survive childbirth is not weak.

Women are not weak, they just have different strengths than men. Women can talk about their feelings until the cows come home – most men can't. Women can love and nurture a baby even at 3AM

– most men can't. Women can breastfeed – men can't. There are a lot of things that women can do, that most men cannot.

Conversely, there are some things that men can do that most women cannot. In general, men run faster, jump higher, throw farther, and lift more weight than women. But none of that has anything to do with shooting.

Women need the added protection of a gun, because, in most cases, they are physically weaker than their male attacker. Women are also less aggressive than males. Statistically, we don't see a whole lot of female muggers and rapists out there. It is said that God created man, but Samuel Colt made them equal. Put a firearm in the hands of a woman, and she is equal, if not better, than a man.

Case in point, I just taught a basic CCW class two days ago. There was a female student who had never shot before. In fact, she was terrified of the gun. This is quite common with women, and it's easy to pick out the novices even before the shooting starts. This particular woman was no different than other beginners I've taught. She picked up the gun with two fingers and held it out in front of her like she was carrying a bottle of nitroglycerine. It wasn't even loaded yet.

The first thing I do with timid women shooters is make them grab the grip of the gun like they mean it, and squeeze it hard. Shake hands with the pistol, and get acquainted. When we begin shooting, I don't even give them a target. I just say shoot into that big berm over there. I have them rapid fire the gun for several magazines until they loosen up. Eventually, they start to like it; they appreciate the feel of power in their hands. In that, men and women are alike.

They almost always put the gun out in front of them as far as their arms will reach, then lean their head and shoulders back in the opposite direction as far as they can. I used to wonder why women did that, but now I realize that they are merely trying to get as far away from the gun as possible. They are afraid of it. This never works. I teach them to respect the gun, but never fear it. The gun is your friend, and someday it will save your life.

However, once a woman has overcome her fear of the gun, then it's Katie bar the door, because she's up there on the line blazing away with the best of men. For some reason unknown to me, women, intrinsically, are good shooters. I've been married three times, and women are still a mystery to me. But I love it, and the mystery has an allure like no other.

I like to have husband and wife teams come to my classes. The husband usually tries to teach his wife to shoot, and that rarely works. A woman wants to be treated as an equal, but a husband, especially when he's in teaching mode, tends to treat her a little like a child. I've seen it many times, and most women rebel against that. They need encouragement and confidence. By the end of the class, the wife is usually outshooting the husband, and he has learned a new respect for her. I love to see that happen, and I believe it's good for the marriage as well. The husband has to see his wife as strong and capable or he will not respect her. Conversely, if a woman does not feel treasured and revered, then she will not be happy in the marriage either. Isn't it amazing what you can learn by reading gun books?

I refer to my wife as my back-up. Not because she is inferior or second in importance, but simply because I view myself as her protector. I'm old fashioned that way. She likes it too, so the arrangement works for us. In a deadly force situation, I will probably be the first to draw my firearm, then while the bad guy is shooting me, my wife will have time to gun him down. But I have every confidence in her abilities, and I suspect that someday she'll save my life or the lives of our children. She's a good woman with a Smith & Wesson. What a deadly combination!

But when it comes to choosing a firearm, women have special needs. Most self defense experts agree that a person should carry the highest caliber they can safely and effectively shoot. For an 87-year-old women with arthritis, that might be a .22 revolver. That's okay. Better to shoot small bullets then none at all.

I once had one of my students (a male) laugh at one of my other students (a female). She had chosen a .22 caliber revolver to carry. He said, "What are you going to do with that little thing, piss somebody off?" His comment rankled me. I quickly replied, "Well, why don't you hold up your hand and we'll fire a few rounds into it and see what happens." He shut up.

Eventually, that same woman decided to get a higher caliber, but the .22 gave her confidence and set her on the right path. Even though she was capable of shooting a higher caliber, it was a good "initial" first choice for her. I remember hearing the story of a woman who was raped. The man was very large and was lying on top of her. She emptied her gun into his torso, but he finished raping her before he died.

For a lot of women, I recommend a .38 revolver with +P ammo. They only hold 5 shots, but they pack a pretty good punch at short range. Since there is no such thing as a long distance rape, this usually does the job. Even the horniest of men will find several Hydrashock rounds in .38 caliber +P to be a powerful mood-altering experience. Kind of like the mother of all cold showers.

Most men prefer to carry semi-autos, but that has more to do with the way we think. Remember the sitcom *Home Improvement* starring Tim Allen? He played the part of your stereotypical male. Bigger is better. Faster is better. Stronger is better. Anything that blows up, catches on fire, or makes a really loud noise is good. But do we really need a lawn mower with a Corvette racing engine? Probably not, but men are creatures of overkill. According to FBI crime statistics, the average firefight remains three shots, three yards, and three seconds. So, according to the FBI, a five-shot revolver is sufficient.

For the actual carrying of the gun, I recommend either a concealment purse or a fanny pack. My wife uses both methods, because they allow her to keep her hand on the pistol while walking to her car in a dimly lit parking lot at night. If need be, she can even fire her pistol without drawing it. I always caution women about leaving their purse unattended in shopping carts. Remember, you are morally, civilly, and potentially criminally liable for any harm caused by your gun should someone steal it while it's unattended. Also, sometimes children get into their mother's purse, so you must be careful about that as well.

In short, women have greater need of a firearm, because they are at greater risk. Most honest, law-abiding men will never be raped, but women have no such reassurance. Wolves prey upon the physically weakest in the herd. In most cases, this is a woman, the young, the handicapped, or the elderly. But if you get training, arm yourself, and be prepared, you can give that wolf the surprise of his life – the last surprise of his life.

So I encourage women everywhere to stand up to criminals. Don't walk around in helpless fear. Arm yourselves, and help us men take out the trash!

When I'm sitting in the McDonald's playroom, and a man walks in brandishing a gun, his life is forfeit. I will kill that man as quickly as possible. To do anything less is to violate the will of God and the nature of my own humanity.

Christianity and Killing

Before writing this chapter, I did a lot of research. But in the end, I threw it all away. Research can be skewed, and statistics can be taken out of context. Instead, I'll just tell you what I believe and you can just take it with a grain of salt.

I believe that when it comes to religion, people will always disagree, so why should I add my two cents to the mess and complicate it even more? Have you ever noticed there are hundreds of Christian denominations, all claiming to have divine Truth? Intrinsic to that, if only one of them is right, then the others must be wrong. They contradict each other, so how can they all be right? The only sensible answer is this – they can't.

I'll speak mainly to Christians here, simply because America is predominantly Christian. I define Christian as someone who follows after Christ and tries to live his life according to the teachings of Jesus Christ. But beyond that, I leave it pretty loose. The gospel of Christ teaches that greater love has no man than to lay down his life for his friend. After all, that's what Jesus did for us. His life, death, and resurrection are crux and core to Christianity. I like Christianity because it is the only major world religion which allows me to have a personal, one-on-one relationship with the creator of the universe.

I may step on a few toes here, but that's okay. God knows that I mean no harm, and He will judge me by the intent of my heart. I'm so glad that He's God and we're not. That's one of the things I like about him, he knows me inside and out, and he cares about me as a person. He's the world's greatest father. (You see, I've already offended the feminists, because they think God is a woman.)

I don't like all these different denominations. There is only one gospel, one Truth, but people just like to disagree, and they can't leave simple things well enough alone. Some people say God is one person, while others argue that he is three in one (a trinity). Some people insist that the Sabbath is on Saturday instead of on Sunday. Others argue about the end times, (i.e., when will the church be taken up to Heaven). Will it be before the great tribulation, during it, or after it? Christians argue about eschatology, demonology, hamartiology, and angelology. All these "ologies" keep trying to clutter up the simple Truth of God's love. I don't like that, and I think we should just cut through all the crap and get back to the basics of Christianity. God loves us so much that He sent His son, Jesus Christ, to die on the cross in our place so that we could live.

It doesn't matter which day is the original Sabbath. Just pick a day and keep it holy. It doesn't matter if God is three or one. He knows who he is and that's what matters to me. Do I have a guardian angel? I don't know. I'd like to. (If I do, then he's not speaking to me lately.) I don't worry about the rapture or the great tribulation. It doesn't matter to me. Besides, I'll find out when it happens and not a moment before. My job is to keep my heart ready at all times and not be surprised when Christ returns. I'm a simple man, and I take simple views on everything. Greater men than me all disagree, and they can't all be right. So I may as well make up my own mind, because after all, in the end, God is going to judge me on what I choose. The experts will be made low, regardless of their claims. There is only one expert: God. Everyone else is just taking their best guess.

I'm the same way about the philosophy of personal defense. I've done a lot of talking these past 170 pages or so, but I don't know any more than the next guy. For all you know, I could be full of crap clear up to my eyebrows. I won't be offended if you disagree with me. Just read it, take what makes sense to you, and disregard the rest. People claiming to be experts worry me. I will never presume to know the mind of God. I'd like to know, and I'll always strive to know, but, in the end, it's still my single opinion, my one tiny, little voice, crying out in the wilderness with no more weight than anyone else's. I like the Crocodile Dundee approach to God: "Me and God. We be mates."

Yes, I am a simple-minded man, perhaps too simple, but it works for me, and I've always been a very practical person. If something doesn't work, then I have no use for it. I'm not a pacifist, and I'm not a bloodthirsty warrior. I'm in the middle. When I'm attacked, then I defend. I don't believe God has any problems with that. I believe that self defense is consistent with God's character, with the works of his hands, and with everything Jesus said in the Bible.

But some of you are quick to quote scripture, to say, "What about turn the other cheek? What about love your enemies?" Those are both good questions. Bottom line for me is this: I don't believe that God lacks common sense. He knows what works for us and what doesn't, because he designed us and knows our thoughts and feelings. I may not know the mind of God, but I do know the mind of man.

There are sheep; there are sheepdogs; there are wolves. No place in the Bible do I see where God would prefer us to quietly be slaughtered. (The Jews already tried that and it didn't work.) I see many hypocrites today on the subject of using deadly force to protect one's self.

For example, the Roman Catholic church teaches in section 2264 of the catechism:

"Love toward oneself remains a fundamental principle of morality. Therefore, it is legitimate to insist on one's own right to life. Someone who defends his life is not guilty of murder even if he is forced to deal his aggressor a lethal blow."

But here in Michigan, the Catholic church came out against the concealed carry bill; they actively lobbied against its passage. How can you teach the moral use of deadly force, but then try to deny people the means to employ it in self defense. This is inconsistent.

And what about the fundamentalists, the so-called right-wing fringe, who insist that human life begins at conception. They claim that abortion is murder, and that the life of that baby should be protected. I agree with them. But some of them would argue for the innocent life of an unborn baby, while simultaneously insisting that the rest of us walk around unarmed, without the means to protect other innocent life, whether it be a child or an adult. This, too, is inconsistent, a chasing after the wind.

Innocent life is innocent life, and all innocent life is worthy of protection. There is a time and a purpose for everything under heaven. I make it a point to stay clear of beliefs that don't employ common sense or which are inconsistent.

Every once in a while, I'll have a Christian come to me and say, "God came to me and told me that you should be doing . . . ."

You fill in the blank, because it doesn't really matter what they tell me. My answer is always the same. "That's odd, God didn't tell me that." I have learned to make up my own mind about my beliefs, and I encourage you to do the same. Don't be bullied by pushy, religious people, claiming to have absolute Truth. Because they don't know any more than you do. God is God, regardless of what people say about him. He knows who he is.

We can argue about this all day, but none of the arguments matter. What matters is what works. The rest is all theory and opinion.

When I'm sitting in the McDonald's playroom, and a man walks in brandishing a gun, his life is forfeit. I will kill that man as quickly as possible. To do anything less is to violate the will of God and the nature of my own humanity. I could never, with a clear conscience, stand idly by and watch another innocent life be taken. I could never live with myself afterwards.

Juxtapose that to the pacifist, who would stand beside my child, my son or daughter, your son or daughter, and watch them gunned down in cold blood. I have no respect for the pacifist. They are free to choose their own death, but not the death of others.

I remember seeing a movie called *"The End of the Spear"* in which several missionaries chose to be butchered by primitive natives, rather than to defend themselves. They reasoned that it was okay if they died, because they would go immediately to heaven, but if they killed the natives, the unbelievers would go to hell. I respect that kind of pacifism. However, I suspect that if the wives and children of those missionaries had been present and threatened, they would have chosen a different course of action. It is immoral to allow a defenseless, innocent life to be taken without a fight.

I believe that pacifism to its extreme is sheer lunacy. Examine the words of the most famous pacifist of all.

In June of 1946, when Gandhi was speaking with his biographer, Louis Fischer, he said.

"Hitler killed five million Jews. It is the greatest crime of our time. But the Jews should have offered themselves to the butcher's knife. They should have thrown themselves into the sea from cliffs."

Fischer then asked: "You mean the Jews should have committed collective suicide?"

Gandhi replied: "Yes, that would have been heroism."

Anyone who can't see the lunacy of that mindset is crazy as well. There is no heroism in sheep. They stand on the hill and go "Baa", as they're being slaughtered.

Ted Nugent has made the following statement many times: "To be defenseless is irresponsible."

He is right. Sheep are born and bred for one purpose: to be killed and to have their parts processed into something useful by predators.

If I am a sheep, then I am a hybrid sheep – a cross between a lion and a lamb. I have grown fangs and claws, and when the wolf comes knocking, I start rocking!

No one kills me or my family without a fight.

Yes, I agree with catechism 2264 of the Holy Roman Catholic Church. It is moral to defend an innocent life even if it means killing the guilty. God will not hold this against you.

I suppose that's pretty simple, but like I said, I'm a simple man.

Blood in the Streets

For God has not given us the spirit of fear; but of power, and of love, and of a sound mind.

2nd Timothy 1:7

Spirit of Fear

A while back I was over at a friend's house and he was showing me his incredible gun collection. He had old flintlocks, shotguns, rifles, civil war pistols - you name it, he had it. Inevitably, the topic turned to politics and gun-hating politicians such as the Clinton gang, Chuck Schumer, and Sarah Brady.

And as we talked, it became apparent to me that this man was very passionate about guns, hunting, liberty and the Second Amendment. I'd known this man my whole life, so I already knew that he came from a patriotic, hard-working family held in high esteem in our community. But then I asked him about an article I'd read in my NRA magazine, and he said, "Oh, I don't get that magazine."

I pressed him further. "You are a member aren't you?" His answer both shocked and disgusted me. "No way! I don't want to end up on some government hit list. As soon as I join the NRA, then the government will know I own guns and they'll come after them."

I was immediately revulsed, and I wanted to say something like this:

"You no good, lazy, no-account coward! How dare you desecrate the blood of our ancestors with your apathy and lack of scrotum! You don't deserve the guns you own!"

But I let those thoughts slip on by me into the ages, and said something less caustic, hoping to shame him into action and reality:

"If you're this terrified of your own government, the people you voted for and elected to govern you and your family, then you've got bigger problems than just losing your guns. We all do. You may not want to hear this, but you've just described a communist regime, not the United States of America."

His response was less than I'd hoped for, and he didn't change his mind and he didn't join the NRA. My respect for him has since dwindled. But here's the way I see it. This poor man is under the false notion that if he lays low, doesn't make any waves, and keeps his head down, that somehow the BATF will forget that he has those 33 guns in his closet. The old phrase "out of sight - out of mind" cannot be applied here. And as far as government lists go, think about this one. Have you ever bought a firearm hunting license? If you have, and, if the government is compiling a list of treachery and confiscation, then chances are, you're already on the list. Now there's a government list that must be huge!

So this friend of mine thinks he's being clever by staying off in the shadows. He thinks that by not openly crusading to keep his inalienable right to keep and bear arms, that he is in some way hoping to keep his own gun ownership unnoticed. This will not happen. His own cowardice serves only to ensure his demise and hasten his own slavery. Besides, if he doesn't have the guts to stand up for what he knows to be right, good and true, then he is already a slave.

I am reminded of the Apostle Paul, an expert at learning contentment while in bondage.

Philippians 4:12-13
"I know what it is to be in need, and I know what it
is to have plenty. I Have learned the secret of being
content in any and every situation, whether well fed
or hungry, whether living in plenty or in want. I can
do everything through him who gives me strength."

It is indeed possible for a man living in chains to feel free inside; and that, my friends, is liberty of the deepest, strongest kind. But an unshackled man who cowers within, who sells his soul for a foolish sense of false security; will never be free. He carries his prison with him, and he is a willing participant to his own slavery. That is not just my opinion, but the opinion of all free men who have lived, and breathed, and pumped the blood of liberty before me.

That being said, I choose to be content, minus the chains of slavery.

I for one will not be shackled! I will fight now! I choose to fight the bonds of tyranny at every turn, even in its present form of political subtlety and deception. Why? Because I like to fight? Because I have all this extra time on my hands with a wife, five kids, and three jobs? No! Because I am bound by my honor as a free man, by my duty as an American, by my vow to God and to my country! I still remember the taste of freedom. It lingers on my tongue like a calling muse; like the cool waters of an oasis in the desert, it quenches the fire in my veins and the discomfited spirit in my soul!

God made us to be free! And that is why we must resist every liberal, subversive, incremental attempt to forge, one link at a time, the chains that would serve to bind us and separate us from God and the liberty he has for us. And that is why I fight now rather than later.

As I write, I am reminded and inspired by the great American and patriot Patrick Henry:

"Is life so dear or peace so sweet as to be purchased at the price of chains and slavery? Forbid it Almighty God! I know not what course others may take, but as for me, give me liberty or give me death!"

The means to ensure our liberties are still in place, but they are being rapidly eroded by an out-of-control government determined to carry out their own self-serving agenda. We must get out and vote and campaign and scream at the top of our lungs as loud as we can! WE WILL NOT BE SHACKLED! WE ARE FREE MEN AND WOMEN! WE ARE AMERICANS, AND WE WANT OUR COUNTRY BACK!

Much better to regain our lost freedoms now politically than to be forced into the last resort of our ancestors who shed their blood and the blood of their sons and daughters from behind every tree, rock and shadow.

Fellow Americans and patriots, please join with me now, standing shoulder to shoulder, crying out against the wrongs and injustices of this world. Make your voice heard. And always remember this: "God is on our side, only because we are on His."

I speak in all humility, diligence and the urgency that was once our founding fathers'. Their blood cries out to us! Defend and protect! Safeguard the heritage we bought for you! The torch of freedom has been passed to you. Pass it on to your children!

If you haven't joined the National Rifle Association (www.nra.org) please do so today. If you live in my home state of Michigan and haven't yet joined Michigan Coalition for Responsible Gun Owners (www.mcrgo.org), then don't wait any longer. There are other groups too, such as IowaCarry.org, and "Ohioans for Concealed Carry". Many states have their own pro-Second Amendment group, and if yours doesn't, then go ahead and start one. Get in the fight! Carry your weight. Join in and help the rest of us shoulder the load. Freedom is not a burden, but it is a heavy responsibility.

"In 2007, many citizens of Iowa who have demonstrated their ability to safely handle a firearm and who have never been convicted of a felony or a violent crime still cannot legally carry a firearm ..."
— *Sean McClanahan, IowaCarry, Inc* —

Hawkeye Carry

I was born and raised in Michigan, and I lived there for 49 years. And then the unthinkable happened: I moved to Iowa, away from family and a lifetime collection of friends. I honestly never thought I would do that. I was very happy in Michigan, but what's that old saying: "Life is what happens to you when you're not looking."

I wasn't paying attention, life happened, and when I woke up, I was living in Iowa, surrounded by friendly, downhome people and the tallest corn I'd ever seen. I still miss my friends, my colleagues from MCRGO and TNUSA, and my family in Michigan, along with the trees and the hills, but I am happy here and putting down good, healthy roots.

I remember that when my wife first came to me about an excellent job prospect she had in Cedar Rapids, that I resisted her attempts at persuasion. I didn't want to move. But, like any man in love, she wore me down and I eventually gave in to her charms. However, I didn't go without a fight, and I held on to three key demands: 1) The kids must have a good school system. 2) The hunting has to be good. 3) I have to be able to get a concealed carry permit.

Well, I did some checking, and the schools are good, the hunting is even better, and that left only the CCW situation, which was a mixed bag at best.

Initially, I didn't believe it would be a problem, since I viewed Iowa as a very conservative area. I just assumed that anything rural would naturally translate into pro-gun. I was wrong. In fact, after doing some checking, I came to realize that Iowa was a "may-issue" state, and "shall-issue" was barely on the legislative radar screen. At first, I ruled the move out, but then, quite by chance and with a little help from Google, I stumbled across a wonderul little group called IowaCarry. They are now incorporated and growing, but, at the time of my moving research back in November of 2006, they were just a small online talk forum espousing the dream of shall-issue concealed carry in Iowa. I clung to them like a life raft, floating in a sea of corn.

I quickly became cyberfriends with people named IAJack, Burddog, Pramunitis, ArmedFerret, Terry1810, Charby, robertsgunshop, Reedie, Sieve, SeanM, G.Dave, Hangfire, HKshooter, SFC Stu, Lady27, HK Dan, and 520fd. Now, after 9 months in Iowa, they have progressed from *cyber* friends, to blood, flesh-and-bone *human* friends of whom I am proud to be affiliated. All of you accepted me into the Hawkeye fold, taught me the ropes (still teaching me) and I am eternally grateful. Thank you.

It was through the IowaCarry.org forum that I learned how to move to Iowa and still maintain my right to keep and bear arms. If not for the infamous red-yellow-green map, I may have been unwittingly reduced from armed citizen to unarmed and defenseless subject. I don't think I could have handled that.

But IowaCarry.org quickly taught me that approximately half the 99 counties in Iowa issued CCW permits in near-shall-issue fashion.

This encouraged me. So, using the red-yellow-green map, I plotted out likely places to buy a house within 30 minutes of Cedar Rapids. (The red-yellow-green county code goes like this: A red county is little or no issue; yellow county is limited issue with greater restrictions; green county is near shall-issue with few restrictions.) Linn county was quickly ruled out, but neighboring Jones county appealed to me from the start. It was rural, mostly farmland, plenty of rivers and fishing, lots of hunting land, and plenty of down-home folk who were friendly and accepting. I still remember the first friends we made in Iowa were Claudia and Bernie of the Anamosa Super 8 motel. I still don't know their last names, but last names don't seem so important in a town of only 4,000 people. According to everything I was hearing from my friends at IowaCarry, Jones county was the place to live. However, I wasn't about to leave my CCW future hanging in the tenuous column, so I quickly called up and spoke with Glenda at the Jones County Sheriff's Department. I still remember the conversation.

"No, Sheriff Denniston's not in right now, but I can tell you that he believes that everyone who wants to should be able to carry a pistol for self defense."

Glenda's words were music to my redneck, gun-totin' ears. Wanting more confirmation, I sent Sheriff Denniston the following email:

Sheriff Denniston,

My name is Skip Coryell, and I presently live in Nashville, Michigan. I am 49 and I have lived in Michigan my whole life. My wife is interviewing in Cedar Rapids, and it looks like she'll be taking a job there soon. I've done a lot of internet research and Jones County looks like the place for us. It's rural, downhome, good hunting, good schools, and the people have been friendly. My last concern is the availability of CCW permits in Jones county. My wife and I have had Michigan permits for 5 years, and we'd like to obtain a valid Iowa permit when we move there.

I have been team-teaching all the CCW classes here in Barry county with Sheriff Dar Leaf for the past 4 years and he can vouch for my character and my ability to teach and to carry responsibly. I am also a former Marine. I have just published a book on CCW titled "Blood in the Streets: Concealed Carry and the OK Corral". You can find out more about me by visiting my website at www.skipcoryell.com.

I understand that Iowa is a "may issue" state and that you have the sole and final say in who carries and who does not. In order to help us find a place to live where we'll be happy long-term, please explain your policy on CCW, requirements, procedures, etc. I tried to call you in person, but could only leave a phone message. Please feel free to call me in person. (269)838-5586

Thanks for your time.

Skip Coryell

I remember pressing the "send" button and then waiting. I recall being very anxious about it and coming back to my computer every 15 minutes or so to hit the refresh key. I came back again, again, and again - for 4 whole, agonizing days! I remember hating the concept of placing my ability to protect my family into one man's hands. In Iowa, there is no appeals process, and when it comes to CCW, the

Sheriff's word is final. If he turned me down, then I'd have to live elsewhere.

Finally, on Tuesday, November 21, 2006 at exactly 4:56 PM, Sheriff Denniston sent me the following reply:

> Skip.....
>
> We would be happy to have you and your family move into Jones County. Sounds as though you have done your homework and I have to agree that Jones County is great place. Not only because I'm the Sheriff but I grew up in Anamosa. I am very easy regarding the permit issue and if you bring your paperwork and a letter from your Sheriff I'm sure we can get you going.
>
> Mark J. Denniston

I breathed a heavy, RKBA sigh of relief and smiled. I immediately called my wife and told her it was a go.

I remember when we first moved to Iowa that my wife was excited about all the extra time I would have on my hands. After all, I wouldn't be leading causes anymore, no more politics, no more fighting for the right to keep and bear arms. Her glee was short-lived. Funny how life happens sometimes.

Just a few months ago, I was elected to the Board of Directors for IowaCarry, so I am once again firmly entrenched in the struggle to keep and bear arms, bringing all my experiences with the Michigan fight, to the great Hawkeye state of Iowa.

Since our move here, Sheriff Denniston has read the first edition of "*Blood in the Streets*" and enjoyed it. Since, by Iowa statute, the Sheriff has sole discretion over what training is required for CCW applicants, he invited me to teach all the CCW applicants here in Jones county. I was pleased to accept the offer. And that's how I became a Hawkeye. (I think that's a bird or something. I should look that up.)

IowaCarry will eventually prevail in the struggle for CCW reform here in Iowa, but I expect it to be a hard-fought political and public relations battle. Iowa is different than Michigan. for the most part, the people here feel safe, and they don't want to be reminded that there are wolves out there who would hurt them and their families. I don't blame them. I'd like to live in a perfect world too. But I don't. Iowa is great, and the crime rate is much lower here than in my home state of Michigan. According to statistics compiled by the Center for Disease Control and the Injury Prevention Center, Iowa was ranked as the state with the eighth lowest gun-related homicide rate, per capita, in the country (includes Washington DC). And I have to admit that I feel safer here than I did in Michigan. (Michigan is ranked 24th.) But, according to the same study, violent crime in Iowa is on a slow and steady rise. (For more stats and the history of CCW in Iowa, go to www.iowacarry.org and read the booklet written by Sean McClanahan titled "*Iowa Gun Facts*".)

Note: For the complete story on Concealed Carry in Iowa, go to www.iowacarry.org. Join the talk forum, and become a member of the organization. Help us advance the right to keep and bear arms. Help us make it fair in the Hawkeye state. While you're there, leave us an encouraging word and don't forget to make a small, online monetary donation. After all, freedom isn't free.

Blood in the Streets

When faced with a weapon-wielding madman, I don't hide beneath a desk, cowering in the hopes that he'll shoot someone else and then move on. I don't roll the dice and hope for the best. Instead, I take responsibility for my own defense, and I attack. That's what real parents do.

Virginia Tech Massacre

On April 16th, 2007, Seung-Hui Cho killed 32 people at Virginia Tech in Blacksburg, Virginia. It was the worst mass shooting in U.S. history. All that day and next, I listened to the news coverage and was sickened by the unnecessary loss of life. It was such a dreadful shame. The next day I couldn't take it anymore, and I wrote the essay below called *"Cower and Die - The New American Mentality"*. The next week on April 23rd, I appeared on the *Deace in the Afternoon* show on WHO radio AM 1040 in Des Moines. For two hours I answered questions from Steve Deace and from callers. Since then thousands of people have read *"Cower and Die"*. It remains to this day my most widely read article. I've included it below. The radio podcast of the WHO radio interview can also be listened to by logging on to my website at www.skipcoryell.com. Every time I think of mass murderers and the government officials who enable them, I grow more and more sickened.

I'm a stay-at-home dad and the primary caregiver for our 1-year-old son. Even now, as I type this article, there is a

40 caliber semi-automatic pistol on my right hip. I carry a pistol 24/7, 365 days a year. Sometimes it's a nuisance, but I will never kneel at the feet of a madman and whimper while he shoots me and the ones I love. Instead, I will take careful aim, and double-tap the center of exposed mass until the murderer falls to the pavement, no longer a threat to the innocent in society. When faced with a weapon-wielding madman, I don't hide beneath a desk, cowering in the hopes that he'll shoot someone else and then move on. I don't roll the dice and hope for the best. Instead, I take responsibility for my own defense, and I attack. That's what real parents do. They protect those unable to protect themselves, and they do so aggressively and without apology.

Having said all that, I, too, would have been helpless to stop the killing at Virginia Tech, or Columbine, or Pearl, and even at the University of Iowa. What do these places all have in common that render a normally competent, personal protection instructor impotent? They are all pistol-free zones. I like to call them criminal safe zones, where bad guys can feel safe and free to exact all manner of evil upon us, the unarmed public, upon our unarmed defenseless and innocent children. Our government, in its infinite folly, has disarmed us, then broadcast for all criminals to see, exactly when and where they can kill the most unarmed people. It's like a bowling pin shoot: the government lines us up, and the bad guys shoot us down. And when questioned about this insanity, the legislators and other politicians say; "we're doing this for your own good". I haven't heard that since I was a child. But I've got news for you politicians – I'm not a child any longer, and I know what's best for me. When the government starts making laws that preclude me from protecting my one-year-old son, then it's time I campaigned to replace them. Consider yourself forewarned. The people hired you, and the people will fire you.

Yesterday, a crazed, lone, gunman, executed 32 people at the Virginia Tech campus. Today, politicians (our leaders) are calling for more gun control. Call me daft, but I don't get it. Where's the logic? Isn't one definition of insanity "doing the same thing over and over again, but expecting different results?" We've tried gun control. It didn't work. It failed us, and it failed our children. It failed us at the University of Iowa in 1991. It failed us at Columbine High School. It failed us in Pearl, Mississippi, and now, it has failed us again in Blacksburg, Virginia.

Why is everyone on television acting so surprised? This is logic 101. If you disarm everyone except crazed murderers, then only crazed murderers will have guns. Let's face it, most people don't have the expertise or the guts to disarm a gun-wielding madman.

Forgive me for sounding harsh, but gun control is killing us. It's killing innocent children all across our country, and it's been killing them for decades. Why? Because we don't have the guts to stand up to our politically correct legislators and tell them no! Enough is enough! Stop killing our children! All across America, even in states where tens of thousands of people have been trained and licensed to carry a gun for protection, people are hiding under desks, jumping from 2nd floor windows, and cowering beneath the muzzle of a deranged killer. As a general rule, the people who cower in the face of determined evil, are the people who die in a pool of their own blood. It's time America – it's time to fight back!

But do the people of America still have the guts to stand up against elected officials? I honestly don't know. Are we Americans? Are we men and women determined to protect our families, or have we all become sheep, content to follow the shepherd over the precipice to the jagged rocks below? Columbine and Virginia Tech are not good omens. The victims there were unarmed sheep, who hid beneath desks and chairs, simply cowering before they died. They said "Baa" as they were being slaughtered.

Something basic to our society has to change. It's time to stand up and fight while we still have the means to do so. And if our politicians tell us we can't protect our children in a daycare center, or a post office, or a church, then we show them the door. We vote them out. We recall them. We take out the trash. That's the attitude that America was founded on. Somewhere along the timeline, America has lost it's way, we've lost our instinct for survival; it's no longer "fight or flight"; it's just plain "cower and die".

Where did Americans ever get the idea that they could successfully outsource personal protection? I know a guy who won't trust another man to mow his lawn, because only "he" can do it right and to his own satisfaction. But that same particular, finicky person walks around all day long trusting total strangers, who aren't even present, to protect the one thing he cannot replace – his own life.

A word of caution: don't think that the terrorists aren't watching, because they are, and they're taking notes.

Once they realize that most Americans are nothing but sheep waiting to be slaughtered, then it's Katie bar the door, because every terrorist and his grandma will be over here killing as many American infidels as they can. America has ceased to be the "land of the free and the home of the brave", and instead has become a target-rich environment, the "ignorant and blissful land of cower and die".

The police cannot protect us; it was never so. The police have their place and their job, but it was never their responsibility to be the bodyguards of every man, woman and child in America. That job is a personal responsibility that most of us have forsaken. It is my job to protect my family; that's why they're called "my" family and not "your" family. I feel silly saying things so basic to life and truth, but, sadly enough, these things need to be said. Trying to outsource personal and family defense will always be a losing proposition.

Take responsibility for protecting yourself and the ones you love. Go ahead and outsource your lawn, but no one can protect your family better than you. It's your job! Do it! Don't give in to the "cower and die" mentality. Instead, crawl out from under that desk and fight for your life. It's a decision you can live with.

Your family is counting on you; they are your responsibility and no one else's. Always remember that and take it to heart. You are a sheepdog.

In Closing

I've talked about a lot of tough topics in this book, so if you are still with me, still reading, still soaking it all in, then we are probably of like mind. (I just can't imagine a died-in-the-wool anti-gunner reading this entire book any more than I could read an entire book by Hillary Clinton or Al Gore.) I know people these days are very busy, so I thank you immensely for giving me the time of day. I know that I have very little time as well, and I'd like to read more, but I just can't. So, again, thank you for your time.

A lot of what I've said in this book is just my opinion, and should be taken as such. In retrospect, I suppose I've been a little harsh on anti-gunners in this book. It has been said, that every person has a right to express their own opinion. I agree with that. But let's face it, some people are idiots, and their stupidity and lack of common sense is a danger to the rest of us. However, I do believe that every person has a responsibility to research the important issues and to then form a rational, well-thought-out opinion. Any idiot can talk, even parrots move their beaks and words come out. (Look at some of our Hollywood celebrities.)

Having said all that, I have more respect for a liberal who has taken the time and effort to thoroughly research an idea before drawing a conclusion, than for a lazy moderate who simply raises his finger and follows the prevailing winds. Being educated on the important, world-shaping issues of our day is the only responsible action. Of course, it is my personal belief that anyone who takes the time to research the facts, will, inevitably, come to the "right" (spelled "conservative") conclusion. For all my liberal friends out there who educated themselves and still get it wrong, I still love you. (Hate the sin, but love the sinner.) Just don't make the mistake of basing your opinions solely on your emotions, because feelings change from day to day, and can never be counted on over the long haul. Use the best tool you have – your brain.

If you take away nothing else from this book, please remember this one thing: "Your family is counting on you; they are your responsibility and no one else's." Always remember that and take it to heart. If you are a sheepdog (in my opinion all parents have the responsibility of guarding their flock, i.e., their family) then you have a responsibility to train, research, and learn all you can about the art of defending the innocent. To all of you sheepdogs (law enforcement, military, CCW holders, parents) you should read over the next chapter very carefully. It is a list of places you can go to make yourself better at protecting your family and other innocent people in society (sheep).

And with that, I wish you all the best as you guard the flock. Keep your eyes peeled for the wolf, and when he shows up, well, what can I say? You're the sheep dog. Do what you gotta do. Survive. And thank you for your service to our country.

God who gave us life gave us liberty. And can the liberties of a nation be thought secure when we have removed their only firm basis, a conviction in the minds of the people that these liberties are a gift from God? ... Indeed I tremble for my country when I reflect that God is just, and that His justice cannot sleep forever.

— Thomas Jefferson —

Suggested Resources

Below is my list of books, websites, and schools, where you can learn more information related to protecting yourself and your family.

Books:

Author, Massad Ayoob

"In the gravest extreme "

"Gun-proof your children "

"The truth about self-protection "

"Stressfire—gunfighting tactics for police"

Author, Ted Nugent

"God, Guns, and Rock-n-roll"

Author, Lt. Col. David Grossman

"Stop Teaching Our Kids to Kill: A Call to Action Against TV, Movie and Video Game Violence"

"On Killing: The Psychological Cost of Learning to Kill in War and Society"

Author, Jim Cirillo

"Guns, Bullets, and Gunfights: Lessons and Tales from a Modern-DayGunfighter"

Author, Jeff Cooper

"Principles of Self Defense"

Author, Clayton Cramer

"Firing Back"

"Concealed Weapon Laws of the Early Republic: Dueling, Southern Violence, and Moral Reform"

Author, Robert Dykstra

"The Cattle Towns"

Author, Daniel and Carol Bambery

"A Common Sense Guide to Michigan Gun Laws"

Author, Skip Coryell

"We Hold These Truths"

"Bond of Unseen Blood"

"Church and State"

"RKBA: Defending the Right to Keep and Bear Arms"

Author, Mark Gabriel, PH.D.

"Islam and Terrorism"

"Islam and the Jews"

Author, Steven Emerson

"American Jihad: The Terrorists Living Among Us"

Author, Wayne LaPierre

"The Global War on Your Guns"

Advanced Firearms Training:

Midwest Tactical Training (www.mwtac.com)

Front Sight Firearms Training Institute, Nevada (www.frontsight.com)

Midwest Training Group (Bob Houzenga) Iowa (www.midwesttraininggroup.net)

Lethal Force Institute (Masaad Ayoob) Held throughout U.S. (www.ayoob.com)

American Small Arms Academy (Chuck Taylor) Arizona

(www.chucktaylorasaa.com)

Defense Training International (John Farnam) Colorado
(www.defense-training.com)

Firearms Academy of Seattle, Washington
(www.firearmsacademy.com)

Thunder Ranch (Clint Smith) Oregon
(www.thunderranchinc.com)

Websites:

> *www.secondamendmentmarch.com*
>
> *www.ofcc.org*
>
> *www.buckeyefirearms.org*
>
> *www.killology.com*
>
> *www.packing.org*
>
> *www.mcrgo.org*
>
> *www.nra.org*
>
> *www.tednugent.com*
>
> *www.skipcoryell.com*
>
> *www.jpfo.org*
>
> *www.gunowners.org*
>
> *www.saf.org*
>
> *www.iowacarry.org*
>
> *www.wisconsinconcealedcarry.com*
>
> *www.missouricarry.com*
>
> *www.ccrkba.org*
>
> *www.ohioccw.org*

About the Author

Skip Coryell now lives with his wife and children in Michigan. He works full time as a professional writer, and *"Blood in the Streets"* is his sixth published book. He is an avid hunter and sportsman who loves the outdoors. Skip is also a Marine Corps veteran, a graduate of Cornerstone University, and the Chief Pistol Instructor for Ted Nugent United Sportsmen of Michigan. Skip is the former Michigan State Director for Ted Nugent's organization. He has also served on the Board of Directors for Michigan Sportsmen against Hunger as well as Iowa Carry Inc. He is a Certified NRA Pistol Instructor and Range Safety Officer, teaching the Personal Protection in the Home Course for those wishing to obtain their Concealed Pistol Permits (www.mwtac.com). He also teaches Advanced Concealed Carry Classes for the more seasoned shooter. Skip is the President of White Feather Press and the co-owner of Midwest Tactical Training (www. mwtac.com). He is also the Founder of the Second Amendment March (www.secondamendmentmarch.com)

For more details on Skip Coryell, or to contact him personally, go to his website at www.skipcoryell.com (email: skip@whitefeatherpress.com).

RKBA: Defending the Right to Keep and Bear Arms

Don't cower in the face of crime! Read this book and make your stand. That's one of the themes in Skip Coryell's new book "RKBA: Defending the Right to Keep and Bear Arms".

Columbine and Virginia Tech were not good omens. The victims there were unarmed sheep, who hid beneath desks and chairs, simply cowering as they died. They said "Baa" as they were being slaughtered. Something basic to our society has to change. It's time to stand and fight while we still can. And if our politicians tell us we can't protect our children in a daycare center, a post office, or a church, then we show them the door. We vote them out. We recall them. We take out the trash! That's the attitude that America was founded on. Somewhere along the timeline, America has lost it's way, we've lost our instinct for survival; it's no longer "fight or flight"; it's just plain "cower and die"!

For a sample chapter or to order your signed copy of *"RKBA"*, go to www.whitefeatherpress.com.

Political Thriller by Skip Coryell
"*We Hold These Truths*"

After Hank Simmons caught his wife cheating with his Editor, he fled the hustle and bustle of the big city, and moved away with his four children to a small one-horse town in Northern Michigan. All he wanted was a little peace and quiet, and a safe and happy place to raise his children. Hank bought the local newspaper, and all was well . . . until . . . nine-eleven.

And then the peace and tranquility of small-town America is suddenly shattered when a terrorist cell group from Detroit is infiltrated by FBI Special Agent Richard Resnik. Agent Resnik, hot on their trail, follows the terrorists to Grand Rapids, but he underestimates the leader, Momin Islam, who attempts to detonate one of two nuclear suitcase bombs, and then flees north, with Agent Resnik in pursuit.

Everything comes to a head when Momin stops in Freidham Ridge for gasoline and a simple bite to eat. Agent Resnik is compelled to join forces with Hank and the townspeople as they fight to capture the terrorist and prevent him from exploding the second nuclear suitcase bomb.

Through the course of conflict, Hank and the other townspeople are forced out of their small, secure worlds, and now must look at things in a global way, where black and white no longer seems cut and dried. Read this geopolitical, redneck thriller and find out what happens when the Mideast meets the Midwest.

For a sample chapter or to order your signed copy of "*We Hold These Truths*", go to www.whitefeatherpress.com.

Suspense Novel by Skip Coryell
"Church and State"

It's the not-too-distant future, and in the wake of a nuclear terrorist attack, the President has signed the Freedom from Religion Act, which outlaws any public expression of religion. But what will the President do now that his wife and son are dead and he has converted to Christianity? Will he stand true to his newfound God, or will he buckle under political pressure? It was his lifelong dream to be President, but now he stands poised to lose it all, just for following the convictions of his heart.

Read this geopolitical thriller and see what happens to our country in "Blood of the Saints".

For a sample chapter or to order your signed copy of *"Church and State"*, go to www.whitefeatherpress.com.

Outdoor Thriller by Skip Coryell
"Bond of Unseen Blood"

Evan Novack, nicknamed Bear by his friends, can pull back a 90-pound longbow and shoot the face off a silver dollar at 100 yards. At the tender age of 14 he had already wrestled a black bear and won! Now at age 34 Bear towers over most men, and weighs in at 250 pounds of powerful, backstrapping sinew and bone-breaking muscle. In short, Bear is the envy of every man, woman and child in North Fork. Every mother's son wishes he were Bear … except for Bear himself.

Though Bear's skills and accomplishments are the stuff of local legend, he is daily tortured by his own private pain and sense of overwhelming loss. Six years earlier, Bear had been separated from his five-year-old son during a bitter divorce, but try as he may, Bear has failed to relocate the son he loves more than life itself. However, unbeknownst to Bear, his son is now orphaned and living in a foster home a thousand miles away.

As Bear continues his unrelenting search for his son, little does he realize that his son has already located him and is on his way to North Fork. But tragedy steps in at the brink of reunion, and his son is kidnapped by a sociopathic killer who has vowed to destroy Bear and all he holds dear. It will take all Bear's skill and prowess as a woodsman to track down and save his son from the deranged killer.

In *"Bond of Unseen Blood"*, Bear must prove his legendary status or die trying! Read this exciting, action-packed thriller to see if Bear has what it takes to save himself and his son, while simultaneously winning over the woman of his dreams!

For a sample chapter or to order your signed copy of *"Bond of Unseen Blood"*, go to www.skipcoryell.com.